Group Discussions

Group Discussions

Mark Peterson

LOTUS PRESS
4735/22, Prakash Deep Building
Ansari Road, Darya Ganj,
New Delhi - 110002

Lotus Press : Publishers & Distributors
Unit No. 220, 2nd Floor, 4735/22, Prakash Deep Building,
Ansari Road, Darya Ganj, New Delhi- 110002
Ph.: 23280047, 98118-38000
• E-mail : lotuspress1984@gmail.com
www.lotuspress.co.in

Group Discussions

ISBN: 81-8382-130-8

Printed & Published by : **Lotus Press Publishers & Distributors,** New Delhi-02

PREFACE

Managers today don't rely on one-man army for taking valuable decisions that are to change the course and face of many things related to their business. Group discussions are an effective way of extracting valuable information and ideas from a number of people, who in the course of the session reveal pros and cons of every idea they come across. Besides, group discussions help managers draw out various skills from the employees that would prove beneficial both for the employees and the company.

With this perception, students appearing for MBA entrance exams and those candidates aspiring to gain a good managerial position in a company are required to go through a group discussion round to prove their ability as a sharp candidate who has a sound knowledge base and can pull through any condition, whether expected or unanticipated.

In a group discussion, the candidates are judged for their alertness and knowledge. They have to be prompt and precise to get their ideas across in an efficient manner. However, no matter how much a candidate knows about the topic of the discussion, he should take care that he must not be over confident about himself.

The present book details on the various tips and mantras a candidate should follow to emerge as a winner in group discussion.

Author

CONTENTS

Chapter 1

What are Group Discussions?

A group discussion or GD is a simulated exercise, where you cannot suddenly put up a show, since the evaluators will see through you easily. An interview is a one–on–one discussion and a Group Discussion is many–on–many discussion. If the many–on–many discussion is not managed to make it one–on–many, the results are less than stellar. Sometimes the group discussion is moderated (for example, in news programmes on television) and sometimes it is not moderated (for example, in jury deliberations, in class team projects).

The advantage of a moderated group discussion is that the participant knows what to talk about and when to talk about it – obviously, when prompted by the moderator. The challenge to the participant is to know the subject matter thoroughly and be articulate in responding to questions and arguments. One must become a good listener and be able to support or rebut the arguments from others in the group. Thus, preparation for the participant involves learning the subject matter and anticipating as many questions and arguments as possible. Acquiring content knowledge is a necessary step but not a sufficient step. You have to practice applying the knowledge to various real and imaginary situations/scenarios. It is the combination of acquisition and application of knowledge that is paramount.

Group discussions that are not moderated pose additional challenges. In addition to subject knowledge, one also has to be careful about what to say and when to say it. In such a discussion, just as in jury deliberations, a quasi–leader (that is,.moderator) often emerges as the discussion progresses.

Purpose of GDs

From the point of view of an interview, GD is a methodology used by an organisation to gauge whether the candidate has certain personality traits and/or skills that it desires in its members. In this methodology, the group of candidates is given a topic or a situation. The members are given a few minutes to think about the same, and then asked to discuss it among themselves for 15–20 minutes.

In a broader sense, GDs allow you to exchange information and ideas. They give the experience of working in a team. Often, in work environments, the management draws on the ideas and expertise of staff through group discussions. Such discussions also help the management to acknowledge the staff as valued members of a team.

Group Discussion (GD) is a logical extension of the admission tests to assess a candidate's overall personality. His/her in–depth understanding of the topic, self–confidence, attitude (rigid or flexible temperament) and initiatives in the discussion, presence of mind in crisis management and speaking etiquette are on test.

The strength of a group usually varies between eight and twelve. Unlike the candidates in the written test, the group here is homogeneous in terms of proficiency level, since they have crossed the first hurdle – the written test.

A candidate has to discuss a general topic ranging from socio–economic to political issues in about 20 to 25 minutes to amicably conclude the discussion. One's success essentially hinges on how effectively he or she communicates to deal with the most complex thing in this world, i.e. human relationship. One must accentuate the stronger points and abandon the weaker sections. Self–knowledge, rigorous and sustained practice coupled with awareness of non–verbal skills leads to a winning performance.

Our body expresses different emotions subconsciously. If a speaker is immensely interested in the subject, truly believes in what is said and honestly wants to share views with others, the speaker's physical movements will be naturally spontaneous and appropriate to what is said. Body language has a direct influence on the responses elicited from those around. Therefore, the speaker must be aware of the importance of body language to ensure that there should not be any mismatch with the verbal communication.

Before appearing for a GD, always remember that it can be a big fiasco due to lack of preparation. One should be regularly in touch with national and international current events, debates, programmes on TV channels, articles and editorials in dailies, magazines and news portals to accumulate one's knowledge and consolidate one's views on everything happening around. Unflinching faith, strong commitment and solid implementation plan will see one through group discussions.

What do Companies Look?

A group discussion tests how you function as a part of a team. You will always be working in teams as a member or as a leader. Therefore, how you interact in a team becomes an important criterion for your selection. Managers have to work in a team and get best results out of teamwork. That is the reason why management institutes include GD as a component of the selection procedure.

Companies conduct group discussion after the written test so as to check your interactive skills and how good you are at communicating with other people. The GD is to check how you behave, participate and contribute in a group, how much importance do you give to the group objective as well as your own, how well do you listen to viewpoints of others and how open–minded you are in accepting views contrary to your own. The aspects which make up a GD are verbal communication, non–verbal behaviour, and conformation to norms, decision–making ability and cooperation. You should try to be as true as possible to these aspects.

Some of the personality traits a GD is trying to gauge may include:

- Ability to work in a team
- Communication skills
- Reasoning ability
- Leadership skills
- Initiative
- Assertiveness
- Flexibility
- Creativity
- Ability to think on ones feet

How do GDs Work?

- Normally groups of 8–10 candidates are formed into a leaderless group, and are given a specific situation to analyse and discuss within a given time limit.
- The group may be given a case study and asked to come out with a solution for a problem.
- The group may be given a topic and asked to discuss on the same.
- A panel observes the proceedings and evaluates the members of the group.

Phases of Group Discussions

Candidates appearing for GD sessions can perform various roles. These roles are defined by the various phases in a GD session.

Stage I: Sharing Ideas

In this stage, the candidates:

- State observations, opinions, ideas, etc.
- State agreements.
- Corroborate examples.
- Ask and answer questions to clarify ideas.
- Define, describe or identify a problem.

Stage II: Explore Differences in Ideas

In this stage, the candidates:

- Identify and state areas of disagreement.
- Ask and answer questions to clarify the source and extent of disagreement.
- Restate the participant's position and possibly advance arguments or considerations in its support by references to the participant's experience, literature, formal data collected or proposal of relevant analogy to illustrate point of view.

Stage III: Negotiate, Extend and Modify Ideas

In the third stage, the candidates:

- Negotiate or clarify the meaning of terms.
- Negotiate the relative weight to be assigned to types of argument.
- Identify areas of agreement or overlap among conflicting concepts.
- Propose and negotiate new statements embodying compromise and co-construction of ideas and concepts.

Stage IV: Test and Substantiate Group Ideas

Here, the candidates:

- Test the proposed ideas against supporting information shared by group members.
- Test proposals against existing understanding of concepts and ideas.
- Test proposals against personal experiences.
- Test proposals against formal data collected.
- Test proposals against contradictory testimony in the literature.

Stage V: Finalise and Act on Group Consensus

In the final stage, the candidates:

- Summarise agreements.
- Make group consensus.
- Apply ideas to problems.

A Common Feature

During all these stages, a candidate might also be required to:

- Encourage other members to participate.
- Encourage and allow other members to perform different roles.
- Encourage sharing of different viewpoints.
- Focus discussion on ideas and not personalities.
- Manage and encourage acceptance of the consensus making process.

Candidate Performance in a GD

A participant needs to know what one's objective in the group is. A good definition of your objective is – to be noticed to have contributed meaningfully in an attempt to help the group to reach the right consensus.

1. Getting yourself noticed by the panel is the first implication. Merely making a meaningful contribution and helping the group arrive at a consensus is not enough. You have to be seen by the evaluating panel to have made a meaningful contribution. For this:

- You must ensure that the group hears you. If the group hears you, so will the evaluator. However, that does not mean that you shout at the top of your voice and be noticed for the wrong reasons.
- You have to be assertive. If you are not a very assertive person, you will have to simply learn to be assertive for those 15 minutes. Remember, assertiveness does not mean being bull–headed or being arrogant.
- And most importantly, you have to make your chances. Many GD participants often complain that they did not get a chance to speak. The fact is that in no GD will you get a chance to speak. There is nothing more unacceptable in a GD than keeping one's mouth shut or just murmuring things which are inaudible.
- Participate in as many practice GDs as possible before you attend the actual GD. There is nothing like practice to help you overcome the fear of talking in a GD.

2. Making a meaningful contribution to the discussion is the second important implication. Making just any sort of contribution is not enough. A meaningful contribution suggests that:

- You have a good knowledge base.
- You are able to put forth your arguments logically and are a good communicator.
- The quality of what you said is more valuable than the

quantity. There is this myth amongst many GD participants that the way to succeed in a GD is by speaking loudly and at great length. One could not be more wrong. You must have meat in your arguments.

- Think things through carefully before presenting your comments.
- An important tip is to enter the room with a piece of paper and a pen. In the first two minutes, jot down as many ideas as you can. These will help you in the latter stages of the discussion and would make your contribution meaningful. However, you need to keep certain things in mind while writing down points for the discussion. If it is a topic where you are expected to take a stand, say for example, 'Should US stop the Iraq war?' note down points for both sides of the argument. It will be useful on two counts:
  - First, if you do not start the GD and are not amongst the first five speakers and find that everyone in the group is talking for the topic, then it makes sense to take the alternate approach and oppose the topic even if you initially intended to talk for the topic.
  - Second, it helps to have knowledge of how group members who take a stand diametrically opposite to yours will put forth their arguments. This will also help you to be prepared with counter arguments.

3. The third implication asserts on highlighting the uncommon points. Everybody else will state the obvious. So, highlight some points that are not obvious. The different perspective that you bring to the group will be highly appreciated by the panel. Here are a few tips on being relevant while having a different perspective:

- Be careful that the 'something different' you state is still relevant to the topic being debated.

- Make sure you can you take the group ahead if it is stuck at one point.
- Be prepared to take it in a fresh and more relevant direction.

4. The last implication is that you must be clearly seen to be attempting to build a consensus.
    - Gaining support or influencing colleagues is the mantra adopted by many a successful business leaders.
    - Nobody expects a group of ten intelligent, assertive people, all with different points of view on a controversial subject to actually achieve a consensus. But what matters is 'Did you make attempts to build a consensus?'
    - The reason why an attempt to build a consensus is important is because in most work situations you will have to work with people in a team, accept joint responsibilities and take decisions as a group.
    - You must demonstrate the fact that you are capable and inclined to work as part of a team.

CHAPTER 2

Types of Discussions

There are different types of discussions, depending upon what is the purpose of the discussion and what results are expected of the entire endeavour.

Task-oriented or Group-oriented Discussions

We can sort out discussions into different types, even if the distinctions seem slightly arbitrary. We can say, generally, that discussions are either task-oriented or group-oriented.

In task-oriented discussions, the group is faced with a problem to be solved, a task to be achieved, an issue to be faced or a subject to be learned.

A task-oriented discussion is usually directive or non-directive.

Directive Discussion : In a directive discussion, the leader takes a very strong role in moving the group toward a goal, overcoming obstacles and disagreements, keeping to a schedule, and coming to a right conclusion.

Non-Directive Discussion : In a non-directive discussion, the leader facilitates a group to approach the issue more independently and arrive at its own conclusions.

In a group-oriented discussion, the group is largely concerned with itself and its own dynamic, in contrast to the discussion of a specific theme.

Let's look at these prominent themes.

- A discussion of Indian politics is task oriented. The task is to examine an issue.
- Discussing riots in India is also task–oriented, but with a strong group–oriented element, depending on which approach is taken.
- An exploration of Indian identity is very clearly both group–oriented and task–oriented, handling personal feelings and perhaps how individuals relate to each other in terms of their feelings of Indian identity. But, at the same time, there may be an element of gaining specific knowledge about Indian culture or a particular aspect of Indian life and history, like Hinduism, Aryan invasion, Mughal emperors, etc.

Long or Short Discussions

Discussions can also be either long–term or short–term. That, as much as whether they are group or task–oriented, dictates how you approach a subject:

- In case there are five meetings to discuss Indian politics, you will obviously handle the issue differently than if you had only one meeting to discuss it.
- Your group will not feel comfortable about sharing their personal experience of exploring riots in India in one two–hour meeting, so what can you even do with the subject in that limited time?

A short–term discussion, for example, almost precludes the possibility of approaching the question of Political parties in India in any but an informational manner.

Discussion Routes

There are different ways of conducting a discussion. The manner in which a discussion is to be conducted depends upon the type of discussion.

Parliamentary Procedure

Parliamentary procedure has been found to be an effective means to reach a decision on highly controversial issues. It represents a formal method of following a body of practical rules strictly. For example, a parliamentary procedure could prove result oriented when discussing about an appropriate political party for India.

Lecture Forum

The main purpose of the lecture forum technique is to share information. People who have engaged in some research or investigation or who have some special competence in an area of interest make speeches. The speech is received by the group without judgment and is followed by a period of discussion. Sufficient time should be allotted for discussion, so members can clarify in their own minds what has just been presented. For example, a discussion regarding a suitable network can be conducted through lecture forum.

Round Table Discussion

Round table discussion is used to increase understanding about ways of approaching and investigating a new problem in which all members of the group are involved. A sub–group of the organisation whose task it is to set policy or direction (e.g., the executive committee) leads discussion by breaking the body into small groups so that everyone can participate in the discussion. For example, prospects of a new product to be launched in market would require a round table discussion.

Debate Forum

After a problem has been discussed at length and a particular proposal is being considered for adoption, a debate forum is appropriate. Speeches for and against the proposed policy can help members crystallise their thinking. For example, the issue of nuclear weapons can help bring many facts to surface when discussed through debate forum

CHAPTER 3

Attempting a Group Discussion

Attempting a group discussion needs as much preparation as strategies to emerge winner through them.

Preparation

You may think that you can walk into a group and run a discussion without preparation. Don't try it. Here are some guidelines to thinking through the subject and how to structure your main areas of exploration:

- Know your material. Have more information than you really need, not only in case someone asks an unexpected question, but also to broaden your own background, sharpen your perspective on the issue, and to strengthen your confidence in your ability to manage the subject.
- Take some time and think of questions concerning your subject that most interest you, for example:

1. What do you most want to know about Indian politics?
2. What aspects bewilder and confuse you?
3. Do you think the common people could have changed things in the past?
4. Can you expect a change in future?

The idea is not to ask questions you think you know the answers to. Questions are not meant to be rhetorical, but to help you prepare by probing the subject in as fresh and uninhibited way as possible, and to provide openings that invite more exploration. You may not even directly allude to these questions in your discussion, but write them down and keep them with you. Remember that you cannot emphasise one point enough: the more directly involved and concerned you are with your subject, the more infectious that concern will be to your group.

- Now, ask questions that you think you'd ask if you were a group member. Anticipate every question you can. Again, put the questions on paper. Keep these questions handy, but don't become obsessed with shooting off answers. Use them to broaden the conversation and to provoke thinking.
- Assess how much you think your group knows about the subject. Give a thought to:
  - How much basic material do you need to impart?
  - Will the theme be relevant to your participants?
  - Or must you find a way to make it relevant?
- Keep your own subject specific. Don't bite off too much, or you are likely to get frustrated and lose control of the discussion.
- Pick a modest and attainable goal. This is especially important if you are directive in your approach. Pay attention to:
  - What do you want to be learned?
  - What is the main question you want the group to leave with?
  - What progress should be made in planning?
  - What change in the attitude or behaviour of the participants would you like to see?
  - What specific problem is to be solved in this or later sessions?

And yet, with all this planning, remain flexible. If your plan is going nowhere, and the others are eager and take things in their own direction, let them go. Don't end a constructive discussion just because it doesn't follow the plan you had prepared.

Openers

For many participants, starting a discussion just might be the toughest task. The question remains – How do you get the discussion started? The participants will be watching you, maybe a few with a glint of challenge in their eyes. You've got to catch them at the very start, pull them in, keep the subject moving and challenge their minds. Have a look at these tips:

- There is no set way to do this; you'll find your own way. Use your imagination. Instead of saying, *'Today I want us to examine Terrorism and what it means for us today'*, you might do a little research and open with: *'I don't think I understood what it really meant to loose a loved one until I read the story about one such woman who…'*

  You could relate the story yourself, as this example did, or let it stand by itself. You can choose a story or anecdote that might be far removed from the actual topic for discussion, but if the story has a strong clear moral message you can bring it back to the subject, and thus in an entertaining way you set the tone for your discussion.
- You can use hand motions, word pictures, etc. for a bombastic opening. But be sure the theatricals and charm don't become an end in themselves. You can set up a crisis, a dilemma, into which you thrust the group like, by saying: *'Ever since you gained consciousness, you have been around people whom you loved the most. You had dreams for them and yourself. But, one day you come to know the harsh reality that they are just not there. It took just an ill – fated moment to take them away from you.'*

- Another opening tactic is to pitch your members a question that you know will get a response: *'How many of you have read 1984 by George Orwell?'*
- Then follow it with a curveball: *'And what if I told you that Orwell's 1984 exists today?'* Suddenly you'll see you've got a discussion going!

Removing Obstacles

Your group may be stiff and uncomfortable. There are plenty of ice–breaker and getting–to–know–you exercises. You can conjure up endless variations of them to fit your purpose. Here are some of them:

Timely use and focus. But be cautious.

- An exercise takes time, and you may have limited time and specific material into which to plunge.
- An exercise not directed toward the topic may divert rather than focus the participants.
- Many exercises focus on the dynamics and mechanisms of discussions themselves. Use them if you want to move directly to the subject to be discussed, by concentrating on techniques to move it foreword.

Unsticking the start

You may find that, especially in a more group–oriented topic, the members have difficulty getting started or pinpointing their specific theme. In that case, it would be smart to have a few exercises up your sleeve.

For example, a discussion on exploring Indian culture may be both too personal or too vague for your group to get a grip on. So, instead of forcing the issue on them, back up a few steps and have them do a trigger activity. Have them, for example, choose a famous Indian from history whom they would want to meet (and why), and think of questions to ask him.

You can see how lively, provocative and fun this exercise can be. And you'll find that both you and the participants have a better idea of what Indian culture means to them.

Moving the Discussion

With the discussion off the ground, the leader becomes a jet pilot. There are many separate instruments and indicators to be aware of at once, many lights that might blink, buzzers that might sound, many separate control buttons to push and levers to pull to keep things running smoothly. The leader has to be fully awake, and needs quick reflexes and the skill and confidence to make decisions without hesitation and to know which buttons to push and which tools to utilise. Something new and unexpected always comes up in a discussion, and the leader needs the equipment and the flexibility to respond.

Content Flow Controls

Your introductory activities with your group include several elements:

- Motivate the participants, stir their interest, pique their curiosity.
- Relate the theme to their experiences.
- Channel the discussion so that the material is challenging and within grasp.

Now, the learning really begins:

- Bring in specific information you draw out from members.
- Bring in opinions.
- Draw out opinions.
- Raise dilemmas for them to ponder and stumble over a bit.

You give your members the push and blast they need to ride on their own momentum for a while, and when that runs out, you give them another stimulus. This is especially true in the non-directive discussion, which is allowed to take a free course. You want members to clarify for themselves what the central points are. The members run the group and you are the facilitator, the fan, the spark–plug.

This requires subtlety and timing and the tolerance and flexibility to see that the discussion might run the course you wish. There are two important approaches for sparking constructive discussions:

Brainstorming

Set aside a certain period for airing and throwing out the wildest ideas possible on your theme:

- What would happen if The British East India Company is once again invited to establish itself in India?
- What if an eminent professor declared to your class that India was actually a part of UK Empire?
  - Turn the facts on their heads to see if they give new, suggestive meanings.
  - Play with your theme as a group, throw out random ideas.

The idea is to develop the intuition to sense something important, lying within the openness to all ideas, so no suggestions get thrown out and they should get written up where everyone can see them. When the session ends, see if the group can draw some order, meaning and serious possibility out of the randomness of playful ideas.

Questioning

Encourage questions, all sorts of questions.

- Urge members to have a questioning attitude toward 'facts'.

- Show them how facts have many interpretations.
- Raise questions that bring the point of discussion directly back to the group:
  - What does this information mean to us?
  - What can we do with it?
  - Has anyone's attitude changed?
  - Is here something we are learning that can be put into action?

Refrain from answering questions yourself, but direct them back to the entire group. At various points in the discussion, ask for clarification, synthesis, or summaries that will crystallise the group's thinking up to that point.

Note, however, that these methods need not be confined to the beginning or end of the discussion, but rather at specific points where the focus of conversation might change, or one particular point is finished with, or when the interchange simply begins to sag. They are tools of which you should be conscious and use at the moments you deem appropriate.

Leadership Functions

There are several functions one needs to perform while leading a discussion. Listed below are some more suggestions used to help the leader keep the information flowing smoothly through the discussion, and to keep the content clear, factual, relevant and interesting. In the course of a discussion, it is impossible, of course, to keep aware of all these functions. You'll probably come away from a discussion feeling that you performed some functions well and messed up others.

Go through this list, pick one or two controls that you may feel a little weak on, and make a point during your next discussion to focus, in your mind, as much as possible on just those one or two points.

Have a look at some of these important leadership functions:

1. **Initiate:** Propose tasks, goals, and define the problem to be approached. This can be done at start of conversation and also at various points within it.
2. **Seek information:** Request facts, seek relevant information from members. Make them think about what they know and express that information in as detailed and precise a way as possible.
3. **Give information:** Provide relevant facts and information, and insert provocative, surprising titlists that are relevant. However, remember that the object is not to simply overload the group with information.
4. **Seek opinions:** Ask for expressions of feeling. Request estimations on the theme. Solicit expressions of the value of the theme. Encourage suggestions and ideas.
5. **Give opinions:** Offer possible ways of viewing the issue, the ways others have viewed it in the past. Bring in provocative opinions, short, written excerpts that clearly state a view.
6. **Clarify:** Interpret ideas or suggestions. Clear up confusions. Define terms. Indicate alternatives before the group.
7. **Elaborate:** Give examples. Develop meanings. Make generalisations. Indicate how a proposal might work out if adopted, or what the results of an action might be if followed to its logical conclusion.
8. **Summarise:** Pull together related ideas. Re-state suggestions after the group has discussed them. Offer a decision or conclusion for the group to accept or reject.

Leadership Style Controls

For better or worse, efforts to create constructive content in a discussion do not occur in a vacuum, but in the context of a group of very unique human beings, with all the potential and foibles found in any collection of such creatures. The leader can to some degree control, direct and diffuse the forces ricocheting within the group. You need all your antennae out for this, and to sense what leadership approach and style is best for you to adopt.

Here are some of the considerations:

- What is the nature of the personal relationships in the group?
- What do people feel about each other?
- What are their expectations?
- What are their preconceived notions about working with each other?

The group members will all be looking at you, waiting for you, depending on you. Here are some quick tips on approaching your group and establishing control:

- Be an active listener, repeating information, acknowledging with body language, eye–to–eye contact, and referring to participants by name.
- Reinforce with kind words and use of your facial expressions.
- Speak distinctly and clearly. If you are telling an anecdote, try to make the listeners taste each word.
- Use your body when you talk. Be lively. Make their eyes follow you a little.
- Don't dominate the discussion; it's not a lecture you're giving.
- Sometimes it will be appropriate to share something of yourself – how the theme, or a particular story or detail, makes you think of something in your own experience or feelings.
- Suggest and invite; don't demand.

- Help participants who are groping. But don't grope for them.
- Don't constantly rephrase questions in your language.
- Beware of stagnating on repetitive points.
- Cut off rambling speakers gently: 'That was interesting, now let's hear others.'

Select your Leadership Style

Different groups may require a different emphasis in style on your part. Also, remember that a directive discussion, by definition, requires more control by the leader. In a non–directive discussion, you will need more subtlety and self–restraint. Each style has its advantages, disadvantages and trade–offs. Have a look at the three different leadership styles:

Permissive (Laissez Faire)

- No clear leadership.
- Allows group to go its own way.
- Totally open–ended and non–directive.
- Spontaneous and haphazard communication – people talk when they feel like it.

Democratic

- Group operates through 'chairman' who is often a voted or accepted figure.
- Discussion and decision–making usually channeled through him or his representatives.
- Group takes an active role exerting its own views.
- Group usually takes turns at speaking.
- Topics are chosen, tasks are assigned and roles allocated by them, where possible.

Autocratic

- Discussion leader takes overall control of the talking of group process and decision– making.
- He/she acts, as it were, on behalf of the group (but often may be pushing for personal or ideological goals).

Leadership Style and its effects

Permissive (Laissez Faire)

- **Making a Decision:** Unlikely to reach decision.
- **Member Satisfaction:** Members not bothered either way; may be frustrated.
- **Attitude towards the Leader:** Still trying to work out who took the leadership role!

Democratic

- **Making a Decision:** Takes a long time but do reach an acceptable decision.
- **Member Satisfaction:** Very satisfied with decision–making process. May be annoyed with slow progress.
- **Attitude towards the Leader:** Respect the leader who is fair, open, and prepared to listen.

Autocratic

- **Making a Decision:** Arrive at quick decision.
- **Member Satisfaction:** May be happy with decision, or resentful as the decision is not made by them.
- **Attitude towards the Leader:** Resent leader, but may sneakily admire his/her ability to get things done his/her way.

Group dynamics

Whether task–oriented or group–oriented, your discussion will always deal, to some extent, with the personalities meeting each other in a common forum.

- Every group will have its own chemistry, as well as its own particular rubbing points. That is what human interaction is all about.
  - There may be an immediate click between them, and between you and them. Or there may be tension.
  - They may all seem to think and talk in slow motion, or they may pop like firecrackers.
- The subject matter may highlight certain clashes that might otherwise lie dormant. A discussion on the Godhra riots, for example, would most likely raise some bristles, and all the fine techniques you hoped to employ will disappear in a shouting match.
- Pressure to plan an activity, or to choose a specific course of action, may bring out sharp disagreement. However, you may also find that the very pressure and intensity draw out a rapport, respect and excitement in striving together toward a common goal.
- The above tips on leadership style can help you, but nothing can replace involvement with your subject, and a respect for and interest in each person in the group.
- You will want to create a warm, open, non–threatening climate that encourages group members to participate. Just as important are:
  - Sensitising the group to, and pointing out within the group, aggression, competition, attention–seeking, messing around, attacking.
  - Discussing (when necessary) the sources of conflict and negative behaviour: like belittling, proving, defending, avoiding. etc.

Roles in Group Dynamics

A useful strategy for developing an effective dynamic in your discussion group is to identify task and maintenance roles that members can take up. Here is a list of these roles and the dialogue that might accompany them in a group discussion about the environmental responsibility of foreign companies.

Positive Task Roles

- **Initiator**: 'Let's take a local perspective on environmental responsibility. Maybe a fast–food outlet?'
- **Information seeker**: 'Does anyone know what McDonalds does with its garbage? Does it recycle?'
- **Information giver**: They won a local government award last year for running an environmentally friendly operation.
- **Opinion seeker**: 'Do you think they're really responsible or is it just a bit of good PR?'
- **Opinion giver**: 'I think it's a combination of the two, but at least they're taking the issue seriously.'
- **Clarifier**: 'We need to get hold of McDonald's annual report to get a better picture of what they're doing.'
- **Summariser**: 'O.K. We're taking a local perspective, using McDonalds as our example and we'll have a look at last year's annual report to see in what way they practiced environmental responsibility.'

Positive Maintenance Roles

These become particularly important as the discussion develops and opposing points of view begin to emerge.

- **Social Supporter**: 'We're coming up with some good ideas here.'
- **Harmoniser**: 'Bakul and Tanya have looked at the issue from opposing points of view. Let's see if we can take something from both points of view.'
- **Tension Reliever**: 'This discussion's really dynamic. It's good that we have so many different valid angles on the issue.'

- **Energiser**: 'Hey, the point that Arun made has really got me thinking. Let's explore his idea some more.'
- **Compromiser**: 'Half the group supports Bakul's view and half supports Tanya's. Now we need to formulate a compromise that we can all live with.'
- **Gatekeeper**: 'How do you feel about the issue, Hemant? Your contribution here would be really valuable.'

During an effective group discussion each participant may take up a number of tasks and maintenance to keep the discussion moving productively.

Apart from these positive roles, there are a number of negative roles which are often taken up in group discussion. You should avoid taking up these roles and learn to identify them in other group members. The discussion group may adopt the ground rule that negative role behaviour will be censured by members of the group. Described below are some negative roles to be avoided.

Avoid these Negative Roles

- **Disgruntled non-participant**: Someone who does not contribute and whose presence inhibits the participation of other group members.
- **Attacker**: Someone who acts aggressively by expressing disapproval of other members and their contributions to the discussion.
- **Dominator**: Someone who takes control of the discussion by talking too much, interrupting other members or behaving in a patronising way.
- **Clown**: Someone who 'shows off', refuses to take the discussion seriously or disrupts it with inappropriate humour.

Quick Tips

Finally, do take note of these quick tips to lead the discussion go in the right direction:

- **Encourage:** Be friendly, warm and responsive to others. Accept others and their contributions. Give others an opportunity for recognition.
- **Relieve group tension:** When emotions get tight and tangled, gently pull people apart, trying to relieve the tension with a joke or diverting remark. Reconcile differences when necessary. Explore them if necessary. Emphasise the need to maintain group cohesion.
- **Compromise:** When your own idea or status is involved in a conflict, offer compromise, show a willingness to be flexible and yield a little. Admit error without belittling yourself.
- **Keep gates open:** Attempt to keep communication channels open. Facilitate the participation of others. Suggest procedures which will draw the participation of everybody.
- **Set standards:** Establish and define standards for the group to aspire to regarding:
    - The level of their communication.
    - The level and depth of the discussion content.
- **Test consensus:** Ask for opinions to find out if the group is near a decision or conclusion on a particular issue. See where they stand on a particular point in the discussion, to assess whether the direction or emphasis needs to be changed.
- **Follow:** Go along with the movement of the group. Accept the ideas of others. Serve as a receptive and interested audience.

- **Question:** When someone makes a statement, follow through with questions to draw out as detailed and precise an understanding of the statement as possible – for yourself, the speaker, and the group.

Concluding a Discussion

As a leader, you need to move your group out of the discussion with the same momentum with which you pulled them in.

- Ask members to summarise the points covered. Throw out questions to them:
  - What questions were answered?
  - Which are yet unanswered?
  - Are people intrigued to learn more?
  - What were the issues discussed, problems solved, decisions made?
  - Where does the group go from here?
- In a one–off discussion with any group, the amount of territory you covered within your larger subject is probably limited. Leave them with something provocative that you held back until now: a story, a puzzling question – something to make them think in the context of the larger subject.
- If the group or subject is ongoing, give group members – or let them find for themselves – an idea of where the group will go next. Remember, if the group is ongoing, not everything needs to be neatly tied up. A loose thread with which to begin the next discussion may be just what you need for them to swing back into action.

Groupthink

Groupthink is a concept that refers to faulty decision–making in a group. Groups experiencing groupthink do not consider all alternatives and they desire unanimity at the expense of quality decisions.

Conditions

Groupthink occurs when groups are highly cohesive and when they are under considerable pressure to make a quality decision.

Negative outcomes

Some negative outcomes of groupthink include:

- Examining few alternatives.
- Not being critical of each other's ideas.
- Not examining early alternatives.
- Not seeking expert opinion.
- Being highly selective in gathering information.
- Not having contingency plans.

Symptoms

Some symptoms of groupthink are:

- Having an illusion of invulnerability.
- Rationalising poor decisions.
- Believing in the group's morality.
- Sharing stereotypes which guide the decision.
- Exercising direct pressure on others.
- Not expressing true feelings.
- Maintaining an illusion of unanimity.
- Using mind guards to protect the group from negative information.

Solutions

Some solutions include:

- Using a policy–forming group which reports to the larger group.
- Having leaders remain impartial.

- Using different policy groups for different tasks.
- Dividing into groups and then discussing differences.
- Discussing within sub–groups and then reporting back.
- Using outside experts.
- Using a devil's advocate to question all the group's ideas.
- Holding a 'second–chance meeting' to offer one last opportunity to choose another course of action.

Evaluation

You may want to evaluate the actual dynamics and progress of the discussion within the group itself. Use your judgment:

- You may not have the time.
- It may be superfluous.
- It may invite bickering.
- Such a group analysis and evaluation may be irrelevant, especially if the discussion is a one–shot deal, and highly focused on the subject matter.

But, for yourself, in both single discussions and ongoing groups, it can only help to have a pulse both on yourself and on the group – but especially yourself. Given here are two checklists to help guide your own progress as discussion leader; you can apply the first list to your group members as well, if you are working with them on their dynamics and it is appropriate. The first focuses on the movement of the discussion; the second (in two parts) – on your leadership style and relation with the group.

Make both of these checklists into charts in which each meeting is recorded, so that you can follow your progress meeting by meeting.

You will be surprised at how this steady review heightens your awareness to the different components involved in your discussion leadership.

Again, this is primarily for yourself, after the discussion, and not necessarily to be shared with the group.

Discussion Movement

Parameter	Remarks
How animated was the discussion?	
Who decided how the discussion should be conducted?	
Was the discussion atmosphere cooperative or competitive between group members?	
What exactly was required from the discussion?	
What was its purpose?	
Did the original subject or purpose of the discussion go through any major changes?	

Leadership Style and Group Dynamics – Positive Roles

Parameter	Remarks
Initiated	
Gave examples	
Asked for examples	
Gave information	
Asked for information	
Gave positive reactions or opinions	

Parameter	Remark
Initiated	
Gave examples	
Asked for examples	
Gave information	
Asked for information	
Gave positive reactions or opinions	
Gave restatement of another's contribution	
Gave clarification, synthesis, summary	
Gave constructive comment/ input on group's movement (or lack of it)	
Asked for constructive comment/input on group's movement	
Encouraged, acknowledged contribution	
Relieved group tension	

Leadership Style and Group Dynamics – Negative Roles

Parameter	Remarks
Acted with aggression or hostility	
Made self-confessions	
Showed defensiveness	
Was competitive	
Pleaded for pet idea	
Sought sympathy	
Horsed around	
Sought status, approval, popularity in group	

Chapter 4

Small Group Discussions

Group Discussions need not necessarily have 8 to10 members. Most researchers define a small group as having at least three and no more than twelve or fifteen members. A group needs to have at least three members, otherwise it would simply be a dyad. With three members, coalitions can be formed and some kind of organisation is present. Too large of a group (more than 12 or 15 members) inhibits the group members' ability to communicate with everyone else in the group.

While conducting a discussion in a small group, care should be taken that the group's members are able to communicate freely and openly with all of the other members of the group. Groups will develop norms about discussion and group members will develop roles which will affect the group's interaction. Keep the following pointers in mind while conducting small group discussions:

Goals: A group must have a common purpose or goal and they must work together to achieve that goal. The goal brings the group together and holds it together through conflict and tension.

Decision-Making: Many groups meet to solve problems or make decisions. Such groups are entrusted with the task of effectively accomplishing their task objectives.

Standard Agenda: Reflective thinking involves a careful, systematic approach to a problem. Groups who use reflective thinking to make their decisions make use of a six–step guide called the standard agenda.

Problem identification: Consider carefully what the problem is and what is wrong with the current situation.

Problem analysis: View the current situation as a balance between restraining forces and helping forces. Consider the forces in play in your group's situation.

Criteria selection: Consider the goals of the final decision.

Solution generation: Generate as many solutions as possible. Avoid groupthink by listing many solutions.

Solution evaluation and selection: Measure each solution against the set criteria.

Solution implementation: Enact the chosen solution.

Brainstorming: Another option for decision–making is brainstorming. When brainstorming, group members are encouraged to generate as many ideas about a particular topic as they can. For instance, group members may use brainstorming to generate as many solutions as they can in the standard agenda step. Group members should be encouraged to say anything that comes to mind when brainstorming. Every idea is written down and judgments about ideas are saved until later, when the group returns to all of the ideas and selects those that are most useful.

Nominal Group Technique: Nominal group technique is a group decision–making tool used when the group must rank a set of options. In order to use the nominal group technique, group members work individually to list all alternatives to a problem or issue. Sometimes, nominal group technique is used after a brainstorming session. Then, the group facilitator asks each group member to individually rank all of the options from lowest to highest priority. Finally, the facilitator computes an average score for each idea. The lowest score is the highest priority for the group.

The Final Decision: There are many ways that a group can make a final decision, decide on a solution or come to an agreement. Some of the most popular ways of making the decision include:

- ***Consensus***: All the group members agree on the final decision through discussion and debate.
- ***Compromise***: Through discussion and readjustment of the final plan, group members come to an agreement by giving up some of their demands.
- ***Majority Vote***: The decision is based on the opinion of the majority of its members.
- ***Decision by Leader***: The group gives the final decision to its leader.
- ***Arbitration***: An external body or person makes a decision for the group.

Chapter 5

Classroom Discussions

Class discussions help students to examine, evaluate and share knowledge about a subject matter. They provide an atmosphere for students to create new ideas, view from different perspectives, and improve their communication and expression skills.

While leading a classroom discussion, you need to be well prepared with discussion techniques and strategies to make things work out in a pleasant manner. At one hand where you need to be aware of the knowledge level of the group members, on the other hand you also need to make sure that you are able to encourage all the students into contributing something useful to the discussion.

Before Starting the Discussion

Identify the Objective of Each Discussion

For example, you want to help your students:

- to focus on the subject matter, or
- to relate the discussions with the course.

Select Appropriate Forms of Class Discussion

For example,

- Student's presentation followed by group discussion.
- Assigning readings to students followed by summary presentation and class discussion.

- Conducting group discussion, in which the whole class is divided into small groups of 3 or 4 persons who discuss a topic for a short time. Then, each sub–group reports the results to the whole class.
- Conducting debate.

Set the Room for Discussion

Different room–setting may affect the participating atmosphere

- Sitting in a circle allows everyone to see and communicate with each other.
- The leader may sit outside the circle to observe and control.
- In a large class, students may form different small groups with their own circle.

While Leading a Discussion

Create a climate to facilitate discussion

- State the rules of discussion, e.g., how to take turns, how to interrupt, etc.
- Preview topics and introduce key terms.
- State your expectation and goal of discussion.
- Provide sufficient time for discussion.

Stimulate Participation

- Raise questions for stimulation.
- Call on students who might provide interesting viewpoints.
- Call on students to paraphrase or summarise the issue just discussed.
- Prepare questions, give students a few minutes to write down their answers, and present them to the whole class.

Guide the Discussion

- Summarise the issues just discussed and list out the key points, clarify students' ideas and ask for comments.
- Comment positively about a student's contribution to reinforce the idea.
- Assign a small specific task to a quiet student to encourage participation.
- Avoid any student monopolising the discussion.
- Prevent the discussion from deteriorating into a heated argument.

CHAPTER 6

Common Group Discussion Topics

In a world that is changing every moment, there are several issues that have gained prominence among people at a global level. Whether it is a classroom discussion or a one that follows interviews of school students, these issues come up as topics to be discussed.

Selecting a topic is a way evaluators use to judge participation in Group Discussions. At times, the evaluators give the group the task of selecting the topic and then discussing that topic for a specified length of time.

Try and think of logical ways to select a topic as a group, setting up criteria as the basic for consideration or selection. Some of the criteria that you could use for selection of a topic could be:

- The topic should be general in nature so that all group members are able to speak about it.
- It should be interesting so that it motivates everyone to be involved in the discussion.
- It should be topical, i.e. it should be current so that it is relevant to today's situation.
- It should be such that a discussion is possible, i.e. at least two points of view emerge.

There are roughly four types of group discussion topics:

- Factual speech topics

- Controversial and argumentative issues
- Abstract discussion material
- Case studies

Factual topics for a group are – as the word says – about facts. This is a sample list of speech topics on current issues and facts:

1. Conspiracy is a very common form of political behaviour.
2. The pros and cons of having a credit card.
3. Drinking and driving is dangerous to yourself and others.
4. Passive smoking is equally harmful.
5. The economic boycott can lead to problems.
6. International trade barriers work.
7. City curfews help to prevent juvenile crime and to protect youth from victimization.
8. The U.N. is mainly based on diplomacy and enhancing relationships.
9. Affirmative action draws people to work they never considered before.

A controversial group discussion topic is a speech topic that has many controversies, pros and cons. Keep in mind that all current GD topics are just a sample list of speech topics!

1. Sustainable urban living without the use of excessive natural resources must be our future.
2. Are there extraterrestrials who influence events on Earth?
3. Marijuana has a medical value.
4. Direct mail is a special form of junk mail.
5. The pros and cons of a female President.
6. Online dating chats have nothing to do with a search for a soul mate.

7. Should schools impart sex education.
8. Most people support embryonic stem cell research.
9. Life imprisonment is a good alternative to capital punishment.
10. What is wrong with child labour?

Abstract GD topics are things that cannot be touched, not be easily defined or formulated. Just think in a creative manner and start a vivid group discussion with one of these abstract topics to talk about:

1. The Nostradamus code
2. Bribery in business
3. Computer viruses
4. Bigamy
5. Hidden persuaders
6. Moral majority
7. The Hippocratic oath
8. Political correctness
9. Vegetarianism

The fourth type of GD topics are so–called case studies. You determine a problem and together with the other group members you have to find a satisfying solution. These are small GD topic ideas. Just modify and alter where necessary; these are just guiding light topic ideas:

1. Leadership – What necessary changes are needed in your community organisation and how do you want to lead the process?
2. Malpractice Insurance – Doctors walk out on the job to protest the rising malpractice insurance costs. What to do about it?

3. Work Ethics – Can we shape workers who have the sense that they serve the company ánd community?
4. School Violence – What are the real causes of violence and bullying in Schools?
5. Recycling – Sort out how to make money with recycling.
6. Dropouts – Individual attention in safe schools and smaller classes; is that the way to stop students to drop out?
7. Iraq – What are the best exit strategies?
8. Speech Privacy – What are the best technologies to safeguard the right of free speech privacy on the internet?
9. Minimum Wage – Why should we have a minimum wage or why not?
10. Burnout – Should everybody check his or herself of burnout signs? How?

Apart from the above topics, GD in different fields have different topics. Have a look at common GD topics related to different fields:

MBA GD Topics

- Is India moving away from a secularist state?
- Education in India – or the lack of it?
- What ails Indian sports?
- The age of information.
- Is philosophy just an armchair theory?
- Success is all about human relations.
- Borderless worlds – dream or reality?
- Quality is a myth in India.
- Education and success – is there a correlation?
- We don't learn from history, we repeat it.
- Do we need a global policeman.

- Indian villages – our strength or our weakness?
- Agrarian Economy in India – boon or bane?
- If there were no armies in the world......
- Indian customs – are we in a time warp?
- 'How green was my valley........'. Is nature paying the price?
- Management Education – Is it necessary to succeed in business?
- The role of NGOs in economics and politics.
- NGOs – do they serve people's interests or are they pressure groups?
- Death of socialism.
- Role of women in development.
- Kids today are not what they used to be.
- Casteless India – a pipe dream.
- Should trade unionism be banned in India.
- Repeated elections – should taxpayers pay for it?
- Indian bureaucracy – foundation strengths or colonial hangovers?
- In India, the whole is less than the parts – do we lack in team spirit?
- Generation X – drivers of our future or are they our lost souls?
- Do we need a cut in the defence budget?
- 'Dot.com' companies – is there room for everyone?
- Artificial Intelligence – will man be ever replaced by machines?
- If I were to choose my person of the millennium...
- All the world is a stage....
- When managers become Hamlets...

- If Patel were our first Prime Minister......
- Materialism – have we sold our souls to the Devil?
- You've come a long way, baby – the rise of feminist power.
- Role of ethics in tobacco industry, liquor industry etc.
- Should gambling be legalised in India?
- Are we unfit for democracy?
- Survival tools for the new millennium.
- Examinations – has it killed education?
- Cultural invasion through the air waves.
- Should doctors be tried in consumer courts.
- Abortion and euthanasia – is it morally right for society?
- Are beauty pageants necessary?
- The relevance of Gandhism today
- India and the WTO.
- Did CBI handle the Nithari issue properly?
- Is e–commerce the best thing for India?
- Managerial skills learnt in the classroom can never match those learnt from experience.
- Democracy is hampering India's progress.
- MBA in India is highly overrated.
- Religion is a private affair and should be of no concern for the state.
- Decreasing defense expenditure and increasing social expenditure is the need of the hour.

Social Topics

- Are big dams necessary?
- Films are corrupting the Indian youth.
- A Gandhian state selling liquor is an anomaly.

- Bride burning and dowry may look bad, but are an integral part of India.
- Our culture is decaying.
- We are not serious about saving wildlife/environment.
- The education system needs serious reforms.
- The impact of MTV on our psyche.
- Showing violence and crimes should not be allowed in films and on television.
- Let us legalise gambling.
- The Internet chains have come on the wings of science and technology but are no less restrictive for all that.
- Secularism has become a tool to justify the wrongs done by the minorities.
- Media is a mixed blessing/how ethical is media?
- To fight AIDS, stop being coy about sex education.
- What should India strive for– westernisation or modernisation?

Management Topics

- Is management an art or a science?
- The rush for MBA is really a rush for big money.
- Ethics in business are just a passing fashion.
- The objective of management is to maximise profits.
- Do professional managers have a chance in our family run businesses?
- The Internet is an exercise in hype.
- Is an MBA necessary to succeed in life?
- Family owned business vs. professionally run business.
- Smaller businesses and start–ups have more scope for professional growth.

- Dot com or doubt com?
- Managerial skills learnt in the classroom can never match those learnt from experience.
- Democracy is hampering India progress.
- MBA in India is highly overrated.
- Religion is a private affair and should be of no concern for the state.
- Decreasing defense expenditure and increasing social expenditure is the need of the hour.

Creative Topics

- The wheel is turning round and round.
- If I was the Finance Minister/Prime Minister.
- There is no right way to do a wrong thing.
- Group Task: how can we have Mount Everest in India?
- Do beauty and brains go together?
- When I woke up in the morning I saw…
- A ship docked in harbour cannot face the storms.
- Up the down staircase.
- Just as we have smoke free zones, we should have child free zones.
- Marriage is a social trap.

Economic Topics

- Developing countries need trade, not aid.
- Why do we lag behind China?
- Capitalism is a very flawed system but the others are so much worse.
- Flexibility of labour laws is the key to attracting more Foreign Direct Investment.
- Is the business of business only business?

- In our economic matters, there is an excessive tendency towards the thinking rather than doing.
- Every cloud has a silver lining.
- Can the economy achieve an 8 percent growth rate?
- Is disinvestment really that good for India or is a rethink in order?
- Are co–operatives relevant in today's globalised environment?
- Foreign aid is a dangerous drug that can stimulate in small doses but become fatally addictive in larger doses.
- Modern day sport in industrialised society is an industry, as anything else
- Government should clean its own hands before pointing finger at the private sector for corruption
- Is the NPA ordinance too harsh?
- Reforms have to grow up.
- The future lies with globalisation.
- Is the consumer really the king in India?
- Globalisation versus nationalism.
- Conditional access system for cable TV watchers: boon or bane?
- If India is poorly governed, the reason is that we have designed our system of governance for protecting, if not encouraging, corruption?
- Commercialisation of health care: good or bad?
- For globalisation to succeed in India people must be able to see what is in it for them.
- Is the US economy headed the Japanese economy way?
- Economic freedom not old fashioned theories of development will lead to growth and prosperity.

- Markets left to themselves encourage greed.
- For globalisation to succeed in India people must be able to see what is in it for them.
- Should businessmen run the finance ministry?
- Should important services like transport be left to market forces?
- Is there any point in having a business strategy when the world changes from month to month?
- Is the patents bill good for India?
- Is the business of business only business?
- Globalisation is good for developing countries.
- Public sector being a guarantor of job security is a myth.
- Capitalism is a very flawed system, but the others are so much worse.
- How can business get rid of the bad name that it has earned?
- Government pumping money into the economy is not the solution for our economic problems.
- Business ethics are no longer a luxury for corporates but a necessity.
- How should privatisation proceeds be utilised?
- Is the budgeting exercise of any use?
- Should agricultural subsidies be stopped?
- Will Mumbai's film industry ever evolve into a truly modern corporatised one?
- Will market reforms enrich rich states further, while poorer ones lag further?
- Why do we lag behind China?
- Who says MNCs are superior to Indian companies?
- Why not use a brand index to measure national prosperity?

- What we need to reduce scams is better regulatory bodies?
- War rhetoric is misplaced in a country like India which is trying to globalise its economy.
- Trade can help the poor?
- The power ministry should cut off supplies to all the defaulting SEBs.
- Steal a few lakhs and you're a criminal. Steal a few hundred crores and you become an industrialist.
- Should PSUs be divested through strategic sale or public offer?
- The state is above the law.

Political Topics

- Reserving seats for women in Panchayat has not only been a farce, but has distracted from developing a more genuine voice of women.
- Have the nuclear tests of 1998 benefited or harmed India?
- Voters, not political parties, are responsible for the criminalisation of politics.
- The voters are required to be well informed and educated about their candidates so that they can elect the right aspirant by their own assessment.
- India should go for the presidential form of democracy.

BPO GD Topics

- Is coalition politics here to stay?
- Does India need a dictator?
- What ails Indian sports?
- Success is all about human relations.
- Borderless worlds – dream or reality?
- Quality is a myth in India.

- Will China overtake India in quality?
- India – the back office to the world by 2020.
- Does Indian IT industry need to focus on products rather than services?
- The BPO age – heralding a new employment revolution.
- The BPO revolution and its impact on the society.
- Education and success – is there a correlation?
- Do we need a global policeman?
- Indian villages – our strength or our weakness?
- Management education – is it necessary to succeed in business.
- Kids today are not what they used to be.
- Repeated elections – who should pay for them.
- Indian bureaucracy – foundation strengths or colonial hangovers?
- In India, the whole is less than the parts – do we lack in team spirit?
- Materialism – have we sold our souls to the devil?
- Role of ethics in tobacco industry, liquor industry etc.
- Are we unfit for democracy?
- Survival tools for the new millennium.
- Examination – has it killed education?
- Should doctors be tried in consumer courts.

Engineering and General GD Topics

- Is China a threat to the Indian software industry?
- Role of UN in peacekeeping.
- Position of women in India compared to other nations.
- Environment management.
- Government's contribution to IT.

- India or west, which is the land of opportunities?
- Water resources should be nationalised.
- Balance between professionalism and family'
- Effect of cinema on youth.
- Education in India compared to foreign nations.
- Are studies more beneficial in India or in abroad?
- 'UN's peace activities' and 'America's war on Iraq'.
- Environment – whose responsibility?
- About hockey being the primary game in India.
- Present state of Indian cricket team.
- Advantages of co-education.
- How to deal with international terrorism?
- Should we pursue our policy of dialogue with Pakistan?
- Is peace and non–violence outdated concepts?
- A unipolar world spells disaster for underdeveloped countries like India.
- Is globalisation really necessary?
- What shall we do about our ever–increasing population?
- Corruption is the price we pay for democracy.
- Foreign television channels are destroying our culture.
- What India needs is a dictatorship.
- With media publishing and telecasting trivia, censorship is the need of the hour.
- *Kaun Banega Cororepati* is less about knowledge but more about money and personality.
- Beauty contests degrade womanhood.
- The rise of regional blocs threatens independent nations like India.
- Six billion and one bronze!

- Is dependence on computers a good thing?
- Should the public sector be privatised?
- China and India are similar nations with contrasting ways.
- Is India a soft nation?
- Value based politics is the need of the hour.
- Religion should not be mixed with politics.
- How to deal with high oil prices.
- Our cricketers are not to blame for match fixing.
- Why can't we be world players in industry as we are in software?
- Multinational corporations: are they devils in disguise?
- Should there be limits on artistic freedom (the controversy on fire)?
- Should there be private universities?
- Can banning fashion shows and New Year parties save our culture?
- Public sector is more a hindrance than help to promote socialism.
- Economic betterment of the poorer nations is as important as disarmament to ensure lasting world peace.
- From public sector to privatization as in the UK, is the right answer for India's instant economic breakthrough.
- The doctrine of 'limited nuclear war' is an ill–convinced, ill– logical, irrational and extremely dangerous concept.
- Some simple but effective electoral reforms will enable us to retain the present parliamentary system and ensure the preservation of democracy in India.
- Nuclear war cannot be won and should not be fought.
- Private enterprise and not public sector will contribute to faster and higher economic growth in India

- Inflation is inevitable in our developing country.
- The policy of reservation is a legacy of the British and it has done more harm than good.
- For a marketing post graduate, without prior work experience working in a big marketing firm is a disadvantage when compared with working in a small firm. Discuss.
- Consumerism is destroying the social fabric of Indian culture.
- Free market is a prerequisite for growth.
- Cricket as a national obsession is a detriment to other sports.
- To develop India has to empower women.
- Formulate the government's health policy to control the spread of aids.
- Advertising is a waste of resources.
- Privatisation will lead to less corruption.
- State is the biggest violator of human rights.
- There can never be a classless society.
- Beauty pageants are a marketing gimmick.
- Voting rights to illiterates in India is illogical because it is widely misused.
- Joint family is a blessing in disguise.
- Higher education should be made possible only for those who can pay for it.
- Women cannot successfully combine both career and home.
- Women are good managers.
- Executives should be allowed to form unions.
- Effect of liberalisation on poverty.
- Indians perform better as individuals rather than in groups.
- Business and ethics go hand in hand, or do they?

- Developing countries should spend more on development than on defense.
- Political parties have outlived their utility.
- Is *swadeshi* relevant for India today?
- Money is required to earn more money.
- Foreign trade is necessary for any country to survive.
- Presidential vs. parliamentary form of government of India.
- Technology: the ism' of the new millennium?
- Religion and politics should not mix.
- Trips controversy and the patent act amendment.
- The CTBT.
- State interventions in market kind or mixed economy.
- Science is a boon or bane.
- Is swapping terrorists for hostages an encouragement for plane– hijackers?
- Nice guys finish last.
- All work and no play makes jack a dull boy.
- Individual freedom and civil society.
- Conventionalism and modernity: the ever going debate.
- Should there be a restriction on permissiveness being propagated by the MTV culture and foreign media?
- Marxism and its future all over the world.
- The growing menace of casteism and regionalism.
- Presidential form of government is needed in India.
- Bullet for bullet: is it the right policy?
- Capitation fees should be abolished.
- Brain–drain has to be stopped.
- Business and ethics can't/don't go together.
- Are women as good as men or inferior?

- Nothing succeeds like success.
- The malthusian economic prophecy is no longer relevant.
- Secessionism in the north–east: who's to blame?
- Should India break diplomatic ties with Pakistan?
- Age and youth: experience and young talent.
- East is East and West is where all the action is: Mark Twain.
- Freedom of expression and the state authority.

Chapter 7

Group Leader

A leader has an important role to play in a group discussion. Sometimes, a group is given the task of selecting a leader before the discussion on the topic begins.

Do not brush this aside as an unimportant formality since you are in a hurry to get on with the actual topic. Selecting a leader in a group is as important as discussing the topic. The evaluators give certain weight to the process used to select the leader since that also involves intra group dynamics. A group in a hurry to select the leader often ends up making a poor choice so that the leader and the discussion end up quite different from what they should be.

There are different ways to choose the leader.

- Avoid random voting and arbitrary methods, such as choosing the first member who puts forth his name.
- There should be some logic in your selection approach. One possible approach could be:
  - The group discusses and understands the role of a leader.
  - The qualities a leader should posses are highlighted.
- Participants interested in becoming the leader introduce themselves and convince others that they posses these qualities.
- The group then selects the most suitable candidate.

- You may argue that there will never be enough time for this and that it will interfere with the time available to discuss the topic. However, the process itself gives the evaluators enough information about each candidate.

Role of the Leader

The running of the discussion depends on a great extent on the leader. Some of his responsibilities include:

- Initiate the discussion, i.e. define the topic, lay down the structure, etc.
- Ensure that the discussion is proceeding in the right direction.
- Contribute by introducing new points or bringing up a new relevant aspect so as to add value to discussion.
- Encourage group participation and allow free exchange of thoughts and ideas provided they are relevant.

Leading a Discussion

Group discussions can be organised in a number of different ways. The methods used in a given command will depend upon the local situation as judged by the individual who takes the lead in the planning. In one unit, small and in–formal discussion groups may be preferred, with little use of public speakers. In another, the popular debate forum for a large audience may be desired.

Leading an Informal Discussion

Under thoughtful and effective leadership informal discussion is the best of all methods. This is true because the small and informal group encourages participation by every member. Maximum learning of facts and exchange of viewpoints is possible. Morale is built up in each individual who feels he has had a direct share in the proceedings. Furthermore, the best way to learn is by doing. If, therefore, one of the goals of discussion is training in exploring facts and opinions related to important public issues, informal discussion groups will provide this training for a much larger proportion of group members than the more formal methods suitable when attendance is large.

Informal discussion groups may profitably be limited in size. Give and take of question and opinion between all members normally will not be attained in a meeting of much more than twenty or twenty–five persons. Fifteen or sixteen is an ideal size, though only six or eight are needed for a lively discussion. In order to attain a desired size, it is often practical to organize two or more groups which meet at different times or places. At a large camp where distances are great it is a good idea to hold several meetings at various locations which will enable personnel to attend without having to walk long distances.

A good leader can make big contributions to the success of informal discussion. If he is tactful and friendly in personality, he will probably be able to draw out the best in the men who make up the group. It is a very helpful thing in a lively discussion to have a tolerant leader who accepts a participant's opinion as something to be considered thoughtfully instead of jumping in at once to refute a view that disagrees with his own.

The leader should be able to think quickly and to express himself clearly and with economy of words and time. If he has a good sense of humour, he will be able to ease tension from time to time by joking remarks. The better he likes his job and the deeper his interest in the subject under discussion, the more successful the whole affair is likely to be. That, of course, does not mean that he should adopt an air of artificial heartiness, but rather that he should have a genuine friendly interest in his group and its problems. Such a leader will want to feel confident of himself in handling the particular discussion technique that is used, and he will want to be as familiar as possible with the subject that is chosen for study.

—

These may seem very high qualifications, but it is a rare command that will not produce many men who can meet them. Moreover, it should not be forgotten that skill develops by practice. Sometimes men can be found who already have had practice in leading group discussions. Others will find that their skill will increase as the discussion groups continue. And, even a leader without experience can do a good job if he takes the trouble to prepare carefully for his meetings.

Relation of the Leader with the Group

A discussion leader does not lead by example or attempt to inspire confidence in himself as an expert. He must not be a propagandist. On the contrary, he must himself be an inquirer. He wins confidence in his leadership by his acquaintance with the background of the discussion and by proposing a way to the next step in the discussion. He does not take the next step and expect the other members to follow. He is in essence a good teacher rather than an academic lecturer. A skilful leader opens the discussion with a brief statement of the question and the salient facts related to it. This takes perhaps five minutes. Then, he starts the discussion with a pointed question. He keeps the discussion alive, if it falters, by summarising points made or issues considered and by asking a question that redirects the talk. At the end, he summarises all major points that have been considered, without attempting to state the 'sense of the meeting'.

The leader must avoid the temptation to clinch the discussion with some stated conclusion. He must remember that one of his chief duties is to leave all conclusions to the individual.

The success of a discussion depends upon the thoughtfulness, breadth, and open–mindedness of the talk that takes place — not upon such tangible results as conclusions reached. If an enlisted person is selected as leader, it is wise whenever possible to have an officer present at the meeting. Since off–duty education is a function of command, a representative of the commander should see that the objectives of discussion are attained.

The leader, of course, need not feel that he should never state his own opinion. There are many occasions when he can do so in a manner that will not jeopardise his standing as leader of the group. He expresses his own opinions as the others do when the opportunity occurs, but he is usually more successful in his leadership as he reduces the amount of discussion time which he personally uses.

Many leaders assign the opening statement or final summary or both of them to members of the group — a device which is particularly useful when some group members are even better informed on the subject than is the leader. This is an illustration of how the leader can both simplify his job and get valuable educational results by delegating certain tasks to others. As a further example, at one meeting the leader might ask one individual to give the introductory statement of facts and request a second to take minutes and make the summary which closes the meeting. In this case, the leader would be responsible for the opening question and for guiding the course of the discussion with necessary questions and interim summaries.

Preparation by the Leader

The leader must prepare for each meeting thoroughly. This is far more important than that he be facile in the conduct of the actual meeting. By careful preparation, a leader can do much toward assuring an interesting meeting even if he is not an experienced chairman.

The leader must, if possible, learn in advance the interests and points of view of the individuals in his group. If he can talk informally with them before the meeting, he can learn the general point of view of each and at the same time help each to become acquainted with him. This will tend to break down any stiffness which may be natural in the first meeting of the group.

He must familiarise himself with the subject for discussion to the extent necessary for intelligent leadership. This does not mean that he is obliged to make himself an expert on any subject that may come into his program. To do so would be pretty obviously impossible. But, he must know enough about the important issues to enable him to keep the train of talk on the track and moving forward. Like a good instructor he must not hesitate to admit lack of information. When a question arises, his normal procedure in any case is to direct it to some group member for answer. If no one sufficiently informed is present, he can with a feeling of perfect assurance suggest a source from which the missing facts may be secured.

He should prepare an outline of the course of the discussion as he foresees it. He will, either as part of his outline or separately, prepare a list of questions which may or should be asked. He must not, however, permit his prepared outline to become a strait jacket for the discussion. The actual discussion can be expected to follow a different course from the one planned in advance, but an outline will assist the leader in his personal preparation. It will also help him to distinguish between major issues, which should be developed when they arise, and minor or unrelated issues, which should be quickly passed over.

He must decide in advance whether he will use assistant leaders, and must see that they too are prepared. He must decide whether he will use such aids to presenting his basic facts as a blackboard, charts, diagrams, or other visual aids. He must have any such desired materials ready for use.

Conduct of the Meeting

In describing the duties of the leader much has already been stated or implied about the conduct of the meetings. Here are a few additional details which the leader must have in mind:

- Physical surroundings should be as comfortable and informal as possible. Whether the group is seated outdoors or in a library, day room, service club, or tent, the members should arrange themselves so as to be able to see each other. If the meeting is held indoors, the leader should be careful that the room is properly ventilated.
- The length of the meeting should be rigidly limited. An hour is about the right time. It is better to close a meeting while the interest in the subject is high than to risk boredom by allowing it to continue overtime in order to attain some aim or conclusion preconceived by the leader. It is not necessary to exhaust the subject — and the audience.
- To a newly organised group the leader should announce briefly the procedure to be used; that personalities are not to be discussed and that comments or questions must bear on the subject or be disallowed.
- Stimulating and guiding the discussion is the most important job of the leader during the actual meeting. He should guide almost entirely by asking questions, by briefly citing a specific case followed by a question, or by summarizing. His questions should ask for reasons and causes (why?), for facts (what?), for circumstances under which certain things may be true (when?), for expressions of opinion (what do you think?), and for common ground upon which some agreement may be reached. The leader should avoid rhetorical questions and any questions so obvious that it can be answered simply by 'yes' or 'no'. These usually block discussions.

Occasionally a question requiring 'yes' or 'no' for an answer, however, can be used effectively. A leader, for example, will state briefly a definite position that can be taken with respect to an issue. He will then ask a member whom he points out, 'Do you agree with that or don't you?' The members' 'yes' or 'no' under the right circumstances will start a lot of protests on the part of those who disagree with him, and the discussion would go off to a new start.

Skilful leaders will ask questions only when necessary. Many good questions will come from the group. They should be encouraged by friendly comment like, 'That is a good question. Who can answer it?' The leader usually needs only to start, to change the direction of the discussion, to bring the members back when they wander too far, and to bring out different points of view.

Both controlling and encouraging participation by all members requires understanding and tact. The talkative member should be allowed only his share of the time, and then should be thanked for his statement and reminded that everyone must have his opportunity to speak. The silent member can be encouraged to speak if the leader will ask him a direct question about which he is known to possess information or to hold an opinion. The opinionated member must be led to understand that positions different from his are reasonable and that thoughtful persons do change their opinions. When the anecdotal member launches forth into his personal experience at great length, he must be handled as the talkative member. The impatient member is looking for a quick, cure–all solution and is perhaps too lazy to think a problem through. He needs to be told that the process of discussion consists, not of giving, but of carefully searching for conclusions upon which each individual usually must decide for himself.

- When the discussion wanders too far from the subject or when it gives signs of flagging, it is a good thing to summarise the chief points made up to that moment. The discussion can then be redirected by another question from the leader.
- Announce the subject, time, place, and special speaker (if any) of the next meeting in a series. If a subject for the next meeting has not been decided upon, take the last minute or two to secure suggestions from the group. Find out if the group would like to continue discussing some issue that has been raised, but has not been explored thoroughly during the meeting. Or ask for a show of hands on two or three other subjects which may be interesting to the members.

Encouraging Members During Group Discussions

There are a number of methods you can use to encourage those that participate in GD One technique is to ask a single question and make a request for all the members to discuss it. The members can read the question, and they can tell the other members what they think the question means.

It is best to use open–ended questions, because they will allow the members to think about the topics. Everyone should be allowed to give their thoughts on the question. It is always important to make sure the group stays on topic.

If you notice that members are getting off topic, politely direct them back to the topic that is being discussed. It is also important for everyone to listen, even the leader. They should understand the statements that are being made by members. If they do not, they should ask the member to clarify the point they are making. It is also important to make comments on statements that have been made by the other members. When you respond to a statement that has been made, this can create a domino effect where other members will respond as well and new ideas or solutions can be formulated.

There are a number of guidelines that you will want to follow at the conclusion of the discussion. You should always create a summary about the topic that has been discussed. Ask the members to review the things that have been discussed, as this will allow them to commit the various points to memory. It is important for the members of the group to keep notepads handy where they can write down important points that have been made. One of the common goals of GDs is to brainstorm ideas. When members of a group are brainstorming an idea, there are a number of things they will do.

First, the topic will be given to the group. Each member will think about the topic for set period of time, and will begin coming up with a number of different ideas. The other members of the group should build on the ideas that have already been presented. After the idea creation period has ended, the ideas which have been developed will be organised and reviewed. The results will be shared with the entire group. Brainstorming plays an important role in group discussions, and is excellent for a situation where a group needs to come up with a solution to a complex problem.

When GDs are held, it is important for them to receive encouragement. This encouragement can come from the group leader, or it can come from the other members. It will bring about results that are the exact opposite of what happens when the idea of a member is put–down by others in the group. The group that participates in discussions should behave like a well oiled machine. Everyone should be on the same page. The success of the group, not the individuals, is the most important factor. When members encourage each other, this will build a strong camaraderie that will allow the group to function as one. The biggest problems occur when members discourage each other and promote their own ideas.

Group discussions are successful when all the members respect each other. When someone comes up with a great idea, they should be thanked for their participation. Members who are quiet should be allowed to convey their thoughts to the other members, and the participants who are outspoken should spend more time listening to what the other members have to say. No one member should ever be allowed to dominate the conversation in group discussion. Every member of the group should be given an equal amount of time to convey their own thoughts to the group.

It is crucial for everyone to feel like they are contributing to the discussion. Conflicts should be avoided or reduced at all costs, as they can destroy the ability to the group to move forward and come up with good ideas or solutions. Encouragement gives members the confidence they need, and this allows them to work hard to make sure the group become successful.

Leading a Panel Discussion

A panel consists of a small group of six or eight persons, who carry on a guided and informal discussion before an audience as if the panel were meeting alone. The proceedings of the panel should be the same as those described for informal discussion: volunteering of facts, asking questions, stating opinions–all expressed with geniality, with respect for the contributions of other members, without speech making, and without making invidious personal references. This primary function should occupy approximately two–thirds of the allotted time-say forty minutes of an hour's meeting. The secondary function of the panel is to answer questions from the audience. This discussion method is suitable for use when a relatively large audience is anticipated. The disadvantage of the method is that it confines most of the discussion to the panel itself. The audience listens and is given a chance to ask questions, but for the most part is passive and receptive.

Panel discussions, if well conducted, are usually more interesting to the audience than is the single–speaker forum. They provide sufficiently varied clash of opinion and presentation of facts to give even the quiet members of the audience a feeling of vicarious participation.

Quality and tasks of leadership in panel discussion are similar to those described for informal discussion. The leader must in addition take special care to select panel members who can think and speak effectively. He must also be sure that they prepare themselves to discuss the subject. During the discussion by the panel the leader has substantially the same duties as in informal discussion except that he should keep himself more in the background as chairman of the panel. He can do so because each member of the panel is in reality an assistant to the leader and is responsible for specific contributions to the proceedings.

When the subject is thrown open to the house, it is the leader's job to recognise appropriate questions and to reject those not bearing on the subject or involving personalities. Some questions he may answer himself, but usually he should repeat the question and call upon one of the panel to answer it. By preliminary announcement, the leader may also tell the audience that they may direct questions at particular members of the panel if they choose. In any case, during the question period the leader needs to maintain strict control. On many occasions this may be the toughest part of his assignment to carry off efficiently and with good humour.

While it is customary to confine audience questions to a specific period, some leaders permit questions from the floor at any time. Unless very carefully limited by the leader, this practice may interfere with effective discussion by the panel.

Arranging the panel properly will lend effectiveness to this form of discussion. The members should face the audience. It is important that each panel member adjust his chair so that he can see every other member without effort the chairman will also find that the best places for his readiest speakers are at the extreme ends of the table. He should keep the more reticent members close to, him so that he can readily draw them out with direct questions. If the quieter ones sit on the fringes of the panel, the more voluble members are quite likely to monopolise the discussion.

Leading Single-Speaker Forum

This is a good type of presentation when an individual who is an 'expert' and a strong public speaker can be secured for the meeting. If a series of such forums are to be planned, it will be necessary in all probability to call upon a different speaker for each occasion. Sometimes it may be possible to invite such speakers from nearby universities or professional and other local associations. Often competent specialists may be found among the officers and men of the command.

The single-speaker forum has the disadvantage of presenting for consideration only one point of view-that of the speaker. An occasional speaker may try to explain various positions that may be taken on the basis of the known facts which he outlines. It is nevertheless difficult for him, in spite of the most conscientious effort, to avoid stressing his own point of view more than others. If the audience or any sizable fraction of it fails to agree with him, what follows the speech is apt to be a battle of wits. Such a battle may try the skill and good humour of both the speaker and the leader.

A second disadvantage of the single-speaker forum is that the meeting is based on a lecture. Men hear so many of these that only the best of them get across. This is not to say that the single–speaker forum is a poor method. With the right speaker and under a competent leader, it can be highly stimulating to the thinking of the audience.

The functions of the leader or moderator of a forum consist of the following:

- To prepare himself in advance on the subject.
- To inform the audience about forum procedure—how long the speaker will talk, when the audience may ask questions, what kinds of questions will be recognised by the moderator, and how long the question period will last. An address of twenty to thirty minutes and a question period of about twenty minutes are recommended.
- To introduce the speaker, explaining why he has been invited to speak and stating the question which he will discuss. It is important to tell the audience what point of view toward the question is represented by the speaker.
- To assure good questioning from the floor. Three or four individuals may be planted with specific questions in the audience. Or signed, written questions may be solicited in advance. The first suggestion fits naturally into the question period; the second is likely to make the forum cut–and–dried, though it is sometimes useful.
- To recognise questioners in parliamentary fashion and to restate suitable questions for the speaker. Acceptable questions ask for additional facts, for an elaboration or explanation of some statement already made, or for an expression of opinion.
- To train the audience to stick to the point and to be tolerant of opinions contrary to their own.

Two types of audience members are likely to require special handling by the moderator. The man who tries to make a speech in the guise of a question may be stopped by a request to re–

phrase his question briefly. The man who merely paraphrases what the speaker has already said for the sake of hearing himself talk should be interrupted with a remark that his statement has been covered by the speaker. In general, the moderator will have to help the audience understand its part by recognizing relevant questions and praising unusually good ones.

Tips for Beginning a Group Discussion

Beginning a discussion can put you in jeopardy or put you in command. The opening speaker is the person who is likely to get the maximum uninterrupted time since most of the other participants would be still trying to understand the basic issues of the topic. If the opening speaker talks sense he/she will get the credit, as he/she opened the discussion and took the group in the right direction, and vice–versa he/she may be marked as a person who speaks without thinking and merely for the sake of speaking. He/she may also be marked as someone who leads the group in the wrong direction and does not make a positive contribution to the group.

- As a discussion leader, speak first only if you have enough sensible things to say. Otherwise, keep silent and let someone else start.
- Try and summarise the discussion at the end.
- In the summary do not merely restate your point of view, also accommodate dissenting viewpoints.
- Mention if the group did not reach a consensus. But, remember not to force a consensus unless asked to by the evaluators.
- Forcing a consensus will backfire and may end up working against you.
- It could project you as a pushy person who is not ready to analyse the issues and is more interested in the final result.

- Keep an eye on the intensity of the discussion. Every GD has its highs and lows. Wait for the lows and time your interjection then. However, it has been observed in GDs where if one waits for the lows he/she would never speak. GDs like that are really loud – where even the lows are very high.
- Jump only when the speaker has finished making his point. The success of our interjection depends not only on our assertiveness but also on the receptiveness of others. If you interject when someone else has just begun speaking it is unlikely that he will let you have your way and vice–versa.
- Do not wait too long or you may lose the opportunity. Remember, there are only a few minutes that you have.
- Jump in an agreeable manner. A useful way of starting your interjection is by supporting a point that has just been made.
- People will let you speak if they think you agree with them or you praise them.
- Try starting by saying something positive about the other person's opinion.
- Jump by raising your voice. The most natural way of entering when you find that others are not listening is to raise your voice. This may not be the smartest way of interjecting but it could work sometimes.
- You must be as loud as the situation demands. To be effective, however, you will have to combine this tool with some of the others we have mentioned, as it is unlikely to succeed on its own.

Resolving a Conflict in a Group Discussion

While handling a GD, you need to be aware that conflict is inevitable. Conflict develops because we are dealing with people's lives, jobs, children, pride, self–concept, ego and sense of mission or purpose. However, early indicators of conflict can be recognised. There are strategies for resolution that are available and 'do' work. Remember that although inevitable, conflict can be minimised, diverted and/or resolved.

Beginning of conflict

There are several reasons for beginning of conflict. Some of them are:

- Poor communication
- Seeking power
- Dissatisfaction with management style
- Weak leadership
- Lack of openness
- Change in leadership

Conflict indicators

If you pay attention to certain details of the discussion and behaviour traits of the members, you would certainly come to know of an upcoming conflict. Here are certain indicators of conflict within a group:

- Body language
- Disagreements, regardless of issue
- Withholding bad news
- Surprises
- Strong public statements
- Conflicts in value system
- Desire for power
- Increasing lack of respect
- Open disagreement
- Lack of clear goals

- No discussion of progress, failure relative to goals, failure to evaluate the superintendent fairly, thoroughly or at all

Destructive Conflict

Remember that conflict turns destructive when it:

- Takes attention away from other important activities.
- Undermines morale or self–concept.
- Polarises people and groups, reducing cooperation.
- Increases or sharpens difference.
- Leads to irresponsible and harmful behaviour, such as fighting, name–calling.

Constructive Conflict

It's surprising, but at times, conflict can be constructive as well. This happens when it:

- Results in clarification of important problems and issues.
- Results in solutions to problems.
- Involves people in resolving issues important to them.
- Causes authentic communication.
- Helps release emotion, anxiety and stress.
- Builds cooperation among people through learning more about each other.
- Results in joining in resolving the conflict.
- Helps individuals develop understanding and skills.

Resolving Conflict

Searching for the causes of conflict is essential to be successful in resolving the conflict. Nine major causes of conflict include:

- Conflict with self.
- Needs or wants are not being met.
- Values are being tested.

- Perceptions are being questioned.
- Assumptions are being made.
- Knowledge is minimal.
- Personality, race or gender differences are present.

Reaching Consensus

Groups often collaborate closely in order to reach consensus or agreement. The ability to use collaboration requires the recognition of and respect for everyone's ideas, opinions and suggestions. Consensus requires that each participant must agree on the point being discussed before it becomes a part of the decision. Not every point will meet with everyone's complete approval. Unanimity is not the goal. The goal is to have individuals accept a point of view based on logic. When individuals can understand and accept the logic of a differing point of view, you must assume you have reached consensus. Follow these guidelines for reaching consensus:

- Avoid arguing over individual ranking or position. Present a position as logically as possible.
- Avoid 'win–lose' statements. Discard the notion that someone must win.
- Avoid changing of minds only in order to avoid conflict and to achieve harmony.
- Avoid majority voting, averaging, bargaining or coin flipping. These do not lead to consensus. Treat differences of opinion as indicative of incomplete sharing of relevant information, keep asking questions.
- Keep the attitude that holding different views is both natural and healthy to a group.
- View initial agreement as suspect. Explore the reasons underlying apparent agreement and make sure that members have willingly agreed.

Initiate Interpersonal Communication

Interpersonal communication is the fuel of group work. It gets members oriented, work done, decisions made, teamwork coordinated and so on. Communication is, therefore, one of the primary responsibilities for every group member.

In many cases, the old saying that actions speak louder than words is especially true of group work. Coming to a meeting unprepared, remaining silent for long stretches, constantly being critical instead of supportive – all of these actions speak loudly to the group and will have negative effects upon the group's morale and progress.

Even body language can be a message to the group: sitting at a distance from others, slouching back, crossing your arms, staring at the ceiling or out the window, sticking your feet up on a chair between you and the rest of the group, all these actions cut people off from the rest of the group as effectively as if they had openly insulted the members. If people in your group seem to be conveying some of these messages of non–participation, especially if they consistently behave this way, someone in the group should address the issue in a constructive way.

When misunderstandings occur, remember that communication is a two way street. Problems of communication are just as likely to be the responsibility of the listener as the responsibility of the speaker. When another group member is talking, you should still be fully engaged in the discussion, actively listening. Avoid the bad habits of talking while listening, most of which are the result of putting your own concerns before those of the group. Avoid these:

- ***Pseudo listening:*** Your body language keeps saying that you're listening, but your mind is really somewhere else.
- ***Silent arguing***: As another group member speaks, you

begin to prepare your list of objections. Try to play the 'believing game' more actively.

- ***Premature replying***: You interrupt the speaker before he is finished.
- ***Misplaced focus***: Rather than trying to understand the fundamental idea of the speaker, you start nitpicking on minor details to which you object.
- ***Defensive listening:*** You hear the speaker arguing with you even when the speaker is elaborating on your idea, asking you to elaborate on it or fundamentally agreeing with you. You relate all the speaker's ideas only to your own, instead of considering them in their own light.
- ***Forcing meaning***: You read more into the speaker's words than could reasonably be expected.

When you speak, you can enhance the group's solidarity by speaking from the perspective of the group. While it's appropriate to use 'I' to voice personal opinions, you should be sure to talk about 'we' and 'us' as well. When people use 'you' to refer to the group, it separates them from the others.

A popular writer on groups characterises the perfect group member as, 'The ideal discussant supports the group's decisions. He speaks of 'we' rather than 'I' and 'they'. He accepts a full share of the blame for any group failure and no more than his share of credit for group success. He carries out any task that he accepted as a representative of the group, never accepting any responsibility that he cannot or will not discharge'.

Guidelines to Problem Solving in a GD

Much of what managers and supervisors do is solve problems and make decisions. New managers and supervisors, in particular, often solve problems and make decisions by reacting to them. They are 'under the gun', stressed and very short for time. Consequently, when they encounter a new problem or decision they must make, they react with a decision that seemed to work before. It's easy with this approach to get stuck in a circle of solving the same problem over and over again. Therefore, as a new manager or supervisor, get used to an organised approach to problem solving and decision–making.

Not all problems can be solved and decisions made by the following, rather rational approach. However, the following basic guidelines will get you started. Don't be intimidated by the length of the list of guidelines. After you've practiced them a few times, they'll become second nature to you – enough that you can deepen and enrich them to suit your own needs and nature.

Note that it might be more your nature to view a 'problem' as an 'opportunity'. Therefore, you might substitute 'problem' for 'opportunity' in the following guidelines.

Define the Problem

This is often where people struggle. They react to what they think the problem is. Instead, seek to understand more about why you think there's a problem.

Defining the Problem: (with input from yourself and others)

Ask yourself and others, the following questions:

- What can you see that causes you to think there's a problem?
- Where is it happening?
- How is it happening?
- When is it happening?
- With whom is it happening? (However, remember that you should not jump to 'Who is causing the problem?' When we're stressed, blaming is often one of our first reactions. To be an effective manager, you need to address issues more than people.)

- Why is it happening?
- Write down a five–sentence description of the problem in terms of 'The following should be happening, but isn't ...' or 'The following is happening and should be: ...' As much as possible, be specific in your description, including what is happening, where, how, with whom and why. (It may be helpful at this point to use a variety of research methods.)

Defining Complex Problems

If the problem still seems overwhelming, break it down by repeating first six steps of defining problem until you have descriptions of several related problems.

Further, verifying your understanding of the problems will help a great deal in conferring with a peer or someone else.

Prioritise the Problems

If you discover that you are looking at several related problems, then prioritise which ones you should address first. Note the difference between 'important' and 'urgent' problems. Often, what we consider to be important problems to consider are really just urgent problems. Important problems deserve more attention. For example, if you're continually answering 'urgent' phone calls, then you've probably got a more 'important' problem and that's to design a system that screens and prioritise your phone calls.

Understand Your Role in the Problem

Your role in the problem can greatly influence how you perceive the role of others. For example, if you're very stressed out, it'll probably look like others are, too or, you may resort too quickly to blaming and reprimanding others. Or, you are feeling very guilty about your role in the problem, you may ignore the accountabilities of others.

Look at Potential Causes for the Problem

- It's amazing how much you don't know about what you don't know. Therefore, in this phase, it's critical to get input from other people who notice the problem and who are affected by it.
- It's often useful to collect input from other individuals one at a time (at least at first). Otherwise, people tend to be inhibited about offering their impressions of the real causes of problems.
- Write down what your opinions and what you've heard from others.
- Regarding what you think might be performance problems associated with an employee, it's often useful to seek advice from a peer or your supervisor in order to verify your impression of the problem.
- Write down a description of the cause of the problem and in terms of what is happening, where, when, how, with whom and why.

Identify Alternatives to Resolve the Problem

At this point, it's useful to keep others involved (unless you're facing a personal and/or employee performance problem). Brainstorm for solutions to the problem. Very simply put, brainstorming is collecting as many ideas as possible, and then screening them to find the best idea. It's critical when collecting the ideas to not pass any judgment on the ideas – just write them down as you hear them.

Select an Approach to Resolve the Problem

When selecting the best approach, consider:

- Which approach is the most likely to solve the problem for the long term?
- Which approach is the most realistic to accomplish for now?

Do you have the resources? Are they affordable? Do you have enough time to implement the approach?

- What is the extent of risk associated with each alternative? (The nature of this step, in particular, in the problem solving process is why problem solving and decision–making are highly integrated.)

Plan for the Best Alternative

- Carefully consider, 'What will the situation look like when the problem is solved?'
- What steps should be taken to implement the best alternative to solving the problem? What systems or processes should be changed in your organisation, for example, a new policy or procedure? Don't resort to solutions where someone is 'just going to try harder'.
- How will you know if the steps are being followed or not? (These are your indicators of the success of your plan).
- What resources will you need in terms of people, money and facilities?
- How much time will you need to implement the solution? Write a schedule that includes the start and stop times and when you expect to see certain indicators of success.
- Who will primarily be responsible for ensuring implementation of the plan?
- Write down the answers to the above questions and consider this as your action plan.
- Communicate the plan to those who will be involved in implementing it and, at least, to your immediate supervisor. (An important aspect of this step in the problem–solving process is continually observation and feedback.)

Monitor the Plan

Monitor the indicators of success:

- Are you seeing what you would expect from the indicators?
- Will the plan be done according to schedule?
- If the plan is not being followed as expected, then consider: Was the plan realistic? Are there sufficient resources to accomplish the plan on schedule? Should more priority be placed on various aspects of the plan? Should the plan be changed?

Follow up

One of the best ways to verify if a problem has been solved or not is to resume normal operations in the organisation. Still, you should consider:

- What changes should be made to avoid this type of problem in the future? Consider changes to policies and procedures, training, etc.
- Lastly, consider 'What did you learn from this problem solving?' Consider new knowledge, understanding and/or skills.
- Consider writing a brief memo that highlights the success of the problem solving effort and what you learned as a result. Share it with your supervisor, peers and subordinates.

Quick Tips for Discussion Leaders

A leader has to be mentally active throughout the discussion to lead the discussion in the right direction. Here are some quick tips for discussion leaders:

Be Prepared

The leader does not need to be an expert (or even the most knowledgeable person in the group) on the topic being discussed, but should be the best prepared for the discussion. This means understanding the goals of the study circle, familiarity with the subject, thinking ahead of time about the directions in which the discussion might go and preparation of discussion questions to aid the group in considering the subject. Solid preparation will enable you to give your full attention to group dynamics and to what individuals in the group are saying.

Set a Relaxed and Open Tone

- Welcome everyone and create a friendly and relaxed atmosphere.
- Well–placed humour is always welcome and helps people focus differences on ideas rather than on personalities.

Establish Clear Ground Rules

At the beginning of the study circle, establish the ground rules and ask participants if they agree to them or want to add anything:

- All group members are encouraged to express and reflect on their honest opinions and all views should be respected.
- Though disagreement and conflict about ideas can be useful, disagreements should not be personalised. Put–downs, name–calling, labelling or personal attacks will not be tolerated.
- It is important to hear from everyone. People who tend to speak a lot in groups should make special efforts to allow others the opportunity to speak.
- The role of the leader is to remain neutral and to guide conversation according to the ground rules.

Stay Aware of and Assist the Group Process

- Always use your 'third eye': you are not only helping to keep the group focused on the content of the discussion, but you will be monitoring how well the participants are communicating with each other. See who has spoken, who has not spoken and whose points have not yet received a fair hearing.

- Consider splitting up into smaller groups to examine a variety of viewpoints or to give people a chance to talk more easily about their personal connection to the issue.
- When wrestling with when to intervene, err on the side of non–intervention.
- Don't talk after each comment or answer every question, allow participants to respond directly to each other. The most effective leaders often say little, but are constantly thinking about how to move the group toward its goals.
- Don't be afraid of silence. It will sometimes take a while for someone to offer an answer to a question you pose.
- Don't let anyone dominate, try to involve everyone.
- Remember, a study circle is not a debate but a group dialogue. If participants forget this, don't hesitate to ask the group to help re–establish the ground rules.

Help the Group Grapple with the Content

- Make sure the group considers a wide range of views. Ask the group to think about the advantages and disadvantages of different ways of looking at an issue or solving a problem. In this way, the tradeoffs involved in making tough choices become apparent.
- Ask participants to think about the concerns and values that underlie their beliefs.
- Don't allow the group to focus on or be overly influenced by one particular personal experience or anecdote.
- Either summarise the discussion occasionally or encourage group members to do so.
- Remain neutral about content and be cautious about expressing your own values.
- Help participants to identify 'common ground', but don't try to force consensus.

Use Questions to Help Make the Discussion More Productive

Some useful discussion questions are:

- What seems to be the key point here?
- What is the crux of your disagreement?
- Does anyone want to add to (or support or challenge) that point?
- Could you give an example or describe a personal experience to illustrate that point?
- Could you help us understand the reasons behind your opinion?
- What experiences or beliefs might lead decent and caring people to support that point of view?
- What do you think people who hold that opinion care deeply about?
- What would be a strong case against what you just said?
- What do you find most persuasive about that point of view?
- What is it about that position that you just cannot live with?
- Are there any points on which most of us would agree?

Reserve Adequate Time for Closing the Discussion

- Ask the group for last comments and thoughts about the subject.
- You may wish to ask participants to share any new ideas or thoughts they have had as a result of the discussion.
- If you will be meeting again, remind the group of the readings and subject for the next session.
- Thank everyone for his or her contributions.
- Provide some time for the group to evaluate the group process, either through sharing aloud or through a brief written evaluation.

Be a Good Manager

- Watch who you watch. When someone else is talking, look at the other people in the room instead of at the speaker. This creates a feeling of greater inclusiveness.
- Don't respond to every statement. Wait for others in the group to comments. If no one does, ask, 'Are there any reactions to that?'
- Keep control. If somebody talks too long, cut him or her off with, 'I think I'm losing track of the point you're making. Can you state it in 20 words or less?'
- Step off centre. If you're running the meeting from a stage or podium, you can encourage interaction by identifying a topic, asking a question and then moving away from the centre of the stage.
- Let others answer questions. When someone directs a question to you, redirect it back to the group, 'Before I answer that, let's see what someone else might say.'
- Think 'I,' not 'we'. Encourage people to take ownership of their thoughts and opinions. If someone says, 'We all think that....', ask if literally everyone in the room believes that or if it's just the speaker's personal opinion.
- Use a flipchart to track progress. When you record ideas generated or topics covered, people in the meeting will have a sense of accomplishing something.
- Summarise. Every so often, pause to ask the group, 'Where are we at this point? Where do we need to go from here?'

CHAPTER 8

Elements of a Group Discussion

A discussion has several elements that need to be taken care of to make the discussion a success in all respects. In order to be able to take part in a successful group discussion it is necessary to understand the elements to understand the elements/ features of interaction.

Verbal Communication

Verbal Communication is arguably the single most important influence on how a group operates and what it achieves. Talking and listening are the substance of problem solving. However, the quality of talk cannot be gauged merely by the level of participation. While it is true that in most cases productive group members are the ones who talk the most, at certain time conversational bullies and time wasters too take up a lot of time.

Furthermore, a focus on talking alone does not take into account the importance of listening. Both quality and quantity of participation are important and listening too is recognised as an integral part of communication. Relatively equal participation of all members is necessary so that:

- Maximum ideas are brought up and discussed
- This leads to greater satisfaction amongst group members
- Finally, if there has been effective participation the likelihood of a consensus is also higher.

Non – Verbal Behaviour

Non–verbal messages which are sent without or in addition to words form a major part of communication. Behaviours of face and gestures of the hands and body can very easily befriend or antagonise others. This is true because 65 to 90 percent of emotional meaning is transmitted through non– verbal messages. Facial gestures, physical position, eye contact and tone of voice indicate feelings and levels of interest. For example, boredom is suggested when a member turns away or looks aside when someone else is speaking. Conversely, keen interest is indicated by a member who sits erect, faces the speaker and maintains direct eye contact. Sometimes, non-verbal clues are complete messages in themselves. A nod of the head signifies agreement whereas shaking of the head signifies disagreement

Norms and Conformity

Norms are standardised patterns of belief, attitude, communication and behaviour within groups and grow out of member association. Certain norms of individual behaviour such as being polite, listening to others points of view, not being too overbearing, giving people a fair chance to participate, etc. should be kept in mind while conducting a group discussion.

Power

In the organisational situation, power comes from occupying a position in the hierarchy. Power can also be earned by a demonstration of efficiency and competence in the discussion. It is important to note that all members in our situation have the same amount of power to begin with. But, during the course of the discussion some members earn more power by their ability to contribute more meaningfully thereby gathering the support of others.

The advantage of having power in a GD is that powerful members (those who have earned more power) are the centres of communications in a group – they talk more and most importantly, other talk more to them than to people with lesser power. There seems to be a reciprocal relationship between participation's and power. Interaction of forces within a group system renders peoples with little power to unable to participate, which makes them even more marginal until they break off from the group or become hostile to it. This harms the group, as it eliminates a potential contributor.

Cohesion

This refers to team orientation and the feeling of 'we–ness' rather than 'one–ness'. Generally groups should pull together and agree on major issues such as the 'nature of the task' and the 'goals' they hope to achieve. The options on how to go about achieving these 'goals' may differ and each alternative may be discussed at length but when a goal has to be reached and everyone is clear on that, it will ultimately be arrived at. Cohesion can come about only when:

- Members are willing to sacrifice personal opinions to uphold group norms.
- There are shared needs, interests and goals.

Decision Making Styles

There are three distinct ways by which decision can be made:

- **Consensus:** It means a unanimous agreement by all members. This form of decision making will, in all probability, not be possible in a situation such as ours as it requires too much time (which is not available to us) and may also involve too many compromises (which again may not be healthy).

- **Negotiation:** It involves bargaining among members to build a solution that honours each person's position on particular issues. This form of decision making is less time consuming and makes bolder decision, as all members need not fully agree with the decision. One drawback is that there is a tendency to arrive at piecemeal solutions.
- **Voting:** The obvious advantage of such a decision making process is its efficiency. It is the quickest and most decisive way of settling issues. However, voting may create divisions, polarising winners and losers and generating resentment and frustrations.

Agenda Value

It is applicable to discussions based on case studies. For any type of formal discussion, there must be an agenda or method for handling business. Without a basic structure for discussions, it is unlikely that a group will conduct the kind of systematic thorough investigation necessary for wise decision making. A standard agenda for a group discussion is as follows:

- ***Understanding the charge:*** Why is the group in existence? What is it to do? What form does its output take? What is to be done with it?
- ***Understanding and phrasing the question:*** What precisely is the group to examine or inquire about? What do the words in question mean? Are all the technical words and issues clear to the members?
- ***Fact Finding:*** What are the symptoms of the problems? What is the cause of the symptoms? What is happening that should not be happening? What is not happening that should be happening? Who is suffering from the situation? How badly? What will happen if the situation is not remedied? How much the question be modified in light of fact finding?

- ***Setting Criteria and Limitations:*** What is possible as opposed to what is desirable. What are the legal, moral, financial, practical and logistical limits on decision making? What would a solution look like? What would be happening that is not happening now? What will stop happening?
- ***Discovering and Selecting Solutions:*** What are the alternatives? How does each meet the goals? How do they measure up against the limitations? Which provides more of what is wanted with the least now harm? Which one should be selected? Who is to do what about what, when and where, with what projected effect and how will it be paid for? What evaluation plan can measure the effectiveness of the solution?
- ***Preparing and Presenting the Final Report:*** What must be written down? What must be said? When, where and to whom? How can the final report be most persuasively presented?

Discussion Techniques

People are generally accustomed to viewing discussion as an activity of sitting and talking about a specific subject. However, discussions can be carried on in many creative, dynamic ways which will hold the interest of the participants and arouse their enthusiasm.

Here we offer a number of techniques that will give people new ideas about 'what discussion really is' and enhance communication on topics of interest.

Try them out in a training session – and do also try some of them in your next discussion plan.

The Magic Circle

Participants sit in a circle.

Anyone can start the exercise by posing a problem or question without proposing a solution.

The participant to the left of this speaker then follows by giving a solution to the problem and posing a new problem.

This continues around the circle.

Review: The magic of this activity is that no one is allowed to answer his or her own questions, yet everyone gets to hear a variety of solutions.

Pass the Buck

The leader holds the buck (any object) and says that no one can speak unless he or she is holding it.

Pass it to the next person or whoever raises his/her hand to speak.

Or: Toss it back and forth – the group member must speak when holding it or is 'out'.

Review: The trainer can leave the review to the end of all the communication exercises or engage in a short review immediately.

Here are the questions for a detailed review:

- Did participants look or listen to the person who held the buck?
- How did they feel when they held the buck and had something to say?
- How did they feel when they had a response, but did not have the right of speech?
- How did they feel when they held the buck and did not want to respond?
- Was the passing of the buck haphazard or was it deliberate? If so, in what way?

- What was going on in terms of continuity of discussion and how can we take this on board in our work?

Feedback Sheets

After a group discussion, make up a sheet that sums up the issues, feelings and/or attitudes discussed.

Photocopy it and pass it around.

State if anything was resolved – and what was not resolved. Describe plans for the future, if any were made.

Examples of a possible feedback sheet:

- We discussed...
- The major points of discussion were...
- The attitudes discussed were...
- The different feelings brought out in the discussion were...
- The conclusions or overriding ideas at the end of the discussion were...
- What if anything was resolved?
- What remains to be resolved?
- What did we accomplish?
- What are our plans for the future?

Energiser

Create a committee of four or more people. Three people then volunteer to act as leaders and go out of the room.

One volunteer re–enters at a time and tries to energise the group.

After each has had a turn (without seeing the others in operation), open up a group discussion on the different approaches used by the volunteers.

Which leaders were the most effective and why?

Try videotaping the three leaders in action and playing back for group evaluation.

An Exercise for the Leaders

Role–play the start of a study or discussion unit on any topic of interest.

One person plays the teacher/leader whose job it is to encourage and accept all participants' suggestions without using words of praise.

Review:

- How did it feel to be on the receiving end of this kind of leadership?
- How did it feel to relate this way to participants?
- What is feedback and what role does it play in the group?
- What kind of feedback needs to come from the leader?
- How do we take this on board in our own work?

Talking Sense

For groups who know each other or have met for several discussions.

- Try a discussion entirely in gibberish.
- Although no words were used, discuss what happened:
- Did people assume their normal roles?
- Were some more talkative than others?
- Did some dominate the discussion?
- Which style of leadership did the leader use? Democratic? Autocratic?
- How much impact did emotions or humour have on the discussion?

- How important were hand movements, eye contact and other physical movements?

My View

This exercise is designed to help participants learn to listen to others by asking them to try and assimilate the views of others during a discussion.

The leader chooses a subject which is likely to produce a number of viewpoints among the participants. At the start of the discussion the leader poses the problem. For example, he or she might give two sides of an issue in the Arab–Israel conflict or religious/secular issue.

The leader asks participants to list initial reactions and first points of view on paper. The leader then allows for a discussion bringing out points of disagreement and having participants explain their points of view.

The leader should stresses that everyone should pay particular attention to and note down points of view which are different from their own, by taking notes and trying to understand the other's position.

Once all have had the chance to express their opinions, the leader closes the discussion by saying:

"We are now going to try an experiment. While you may all feel strongly about your views, I'd like to ask you now to look at your notes about the alternative points of view. Do you understand those views? Take a minute to think about the points expressed by others."

After a few minutes the leader asks the group to continue the discussion, this time defending the opinion most unlike his/her own. The discussion, if possible, should continue for about ten minutes or until each member has a chance to defend a new point of view.

Review

The activity can be summed up with a discussion of the following points:

1. Were you able to defend another's position convincingly? Why or why not?
2. During the first part of the discussion did you truly listen openly to the points of others or were you constantly defending and gaining 'ammunition' for your point of view?
3. Is it possible for people of vastly different views to engage in open, honest communication? Why or why not?
4. Were all or some of your views changed as a result of this exercise?

As a follow–up to this activity, the group might be reconvened at a later date to have a discussion of the original issue.

- Are people more willing to listen to each other?
- Is communication greater?

CHAPTER 9

Taking Decisions

Group decision making is the process of arriving at a judgment based upon the feedback of multiple individuals. Such decision making is a key component to the functioning of an organisation, because organisational performance involves more than just individual action. Due to the importance of the group decision making process, decision making models can be used to establish a systematic means of developing effective group decision making. In general, four group decision making models can be identified each possessing distinct advantages and disadvantages. These four models are the rational, political, process and garbage can models.

Importance of Models in Decision Making

Organisational performance is largely dependent upon the decision making processes that a particular organisation uses. In every organisation, decisions have to be made on a daily basis. These decisions range from small to large–scale in scope both in terms of the resources involved in making them and the impact that the decisions can have. For instance, a small–scale decision would be determining the type of copy machine to purchase for a company department. This decision involves resources (i.e., in the form of time and energy) of the users of this machine to clarify their needs as well as the purchasing representatives who research and acquire the copier. The ability of this copier to meet employees' needs decides the impact of this decision.

An example of a large–scale decision would be determining what product or service a company's customers need. This decision involves the time and energy of the individuals who research the consumer market, as well as the individuals who try to successfully develop and launch the product or service. This decision has the potential to make or break a company, depending on the size of the organisation.

As the preceding examples illustrate, the decisions and the processes involved in making them are not limited to the individual level. Moreover, the decision–making process is also performed at the group level, and it will be done so with increasing frequency given the need for high performance organisations in a competitive, global market.

Since the resources involved in the group decision–making process as well as the impact of these decisions affect organisational performance, it is crucial to make the group decision–making process as efficient and effective as possible. Utilising a decision–making model is a systematic way of establishing group decision making proficiency. This statement is not intended to mean that the use of a group decision–making model is a panacea for group and organisational processes. This statement is merely intended to mean that a group decision–making model when used appropriately can aid in the functioning of the group and the organisation.

In order to determine the appropriate use of a group decision–making model, the advantages and disadvantages of using a model should be discussed. The advantage of using a model is that it helps to enhance understanding. More specifically, a model assists in identifying the functioning of a group. It lends structure to a procedure that is dynamic and conceptual. By lending structure, it facilitates the identification and resolution of problems that can arise during the course and as a consequence of the decision–

making process. This facilitation in turn can assist in improving the group decision–making process.

The potential disadvantage or pitfall to be aware of when using a model is that of being trapped by it. Using one particular model should not preclude the consideration of other models or other means of assessing group decision making. If a model is strictly adhered to without being open to other potential ideas, valuable information may be missed due to blatant disregard or misclassification of the information. Therefore, this limitation should be kept in mind in utilizing a group decision–making model.

A multiplicity of models exists regarding group decision making. So, it is not reasonably feasible to discuss every type. In general, there are four basic models of group decision making. Each one has its own assumptions and effectiveness criteria associated with it.

The Rational Model

The first model is the rational model. This model is based upon an economic view of decision making. It is grounded on goals/ objectives, alternatives, consequences and optimality. The model assumes that complete information regarding the decision to be made is available and one correct conception of the problem, or decision to be made can be determined. The model further assumes that the decision–makers consistently assess the advantages and disadvantages of any alternatives with goals and objectives in mind. They then evaluate the consequences of selecting or not selecting each alternative. The alternative that provides the maximum utility (i.e., the optimal choice) will be selected. The rational model is the baseline against which other models are compared.

An example of a scenario using a rational model is an executive group of a company trying to determine which consulting firm to hire in order to implement a business process reengineering (BPR) effort. The executive group's goal or objective is to become a leader in its industry, and it determines that the best way to accomplish this objective is through re–engineering. Numerous management consulting firms offer BPR services. Each firm's BPR approach has advantages and disadvantages. The executive group must evaluate each firm's approach by considering how the firm will enable the company to meet its objective. Based upon this evaluation, the group selects the consulting firm that provides the best means for the company to become a leader in its industry.

The most salient advantage of the rational model is that it utilizes a logical, sequential approach. Decisions are made deductively by determining the goals or objectives to be obtained, evaluating the potential alternatives based on the information at hand and choosing the optimal alternative. In other words, the model is simple and intuitive in nature.

The rational model does possess a salient disadvantage. The model assumes that there are no intrinsic biases to the decision–making process. This optimism may not be totally realistic, since individuals involved in the process bring their own perceptions and mental models into such a situation. Therefore, it seems that intrinsic biases are inevitable and something that should be addressed.

The Political Model

The second basic decision–making model considers the preconceived notions that decision–makers bring to the table in the decision process. This model is the political model. In contrast to the preceding model, the individuals involved do not accomplish the decision task through rational choice in regard to objectives. The decision makers are motivated by and act on their own needs and perceptions. This process involves a cycle of bargaining among the decision makers in order for each one to try to get his or her perspective to be the one of choice. More specifically, this process involves each decision–maker trying to sway powerful people within the situation to adopt his or her viewpoint and influence the remaining decision–makers.

Furthermore, the political model does not involve making full information available or a focus on the optimal viewpoint like that of the rational model. Full information is highly unlikely, since the political model operates based upon negotiation that is often influenced by power and favours. In fact, information is often withheld in order to better manoeuvre a given perspective. Since information is often withheld and subsequently incomplete, the optimal viewpoint is not a key aspect of this model.

An illustration of the political model in action is a decision to hire a new manager for the Purchasing Department of a company. A group composed of the Human Resources (HR) Manager, staff members of the Purchasing Department, and the Director of Operations (i.e., whose division oversees the Purchasing Department) must make the decision among three candidates for the position. Each member has his or her own needs and reasons for endorsing certain job candidates.

The HR Manager is trying to fit the best person to the job, but would not mind if this individual has an innate liking for and understanding of human resources. This appreciation of HR would help decrease the cycle time of placing and receiving orders for necessities. The HR Manager would like to hire the first candidate.

The purchasing staff is also trying to find the best person for the position, but would prefer someone who does not micro–manage like their previous boss. The Purchasing staff would like to hire the second candidate. The Director of Operations also desires to find the best person for the job, but the Director would prefer an individual who unlike the previous Purchasing Manager is not overbearing and sceptical of the Director's decisions. The Director would like to hire the third candidate.

Since the group members have different agendas, they need to negotiate with each other and present their cases to the Director of Operations who has the final say in the decision. In the end, the Director understands the argument of the Purchasing staff and decides that the second candidate's hands–off approach would meet his needs as well. Therefore, the second candidate is hired.

The advantages of the political model remains that it provides a representation of the subjective manner in which the real world often operates, and it can minimise conflict. Individuals will always have their personal biases and agendas that influence their behaviour. By identifying or acknowledging this fact in the decision–making process, potential problems and conflict can be foreseen and minimised. Conflict is also minimised by the swaying of powerful people to support a particular viewpoint. Once the powerful people support this perspective, other group members usually fall in line behind them.

While the political model has the advantage of emulating the way the real world operates (i.e., a cycle of bargaining related to personal agendas), this fact is also a disadvantage, because the best solution or decision may not be selected. Furthermore, the nature of bargaining and manoeuvring (e.g., withholding information and social pressure) can produce effects that are long–lasting and detrimental. Once they discover it, the individuals involved in the decision may not appreciate the duplicity inherent in the process.

The Process Model

In contrast to the political model, the third basic model of decision making is more structured. This model is the process model. With the process model, decisions are made based upon standard operating procedures, or pre–established guidelines within the organisation. Actions and behaviours occur in accordance with these procedures or guidelines.

Additionally, the organisation of past, present, and future events, as well as conformity, are integral parts to this model. The organisation of the past, present and future events are important, because they can be used as a consistent foundation for decision making. Considering these time events provides further refinement of the guidelines that help to determine outcomes.

Conformity is an integral part of the process model since it is the means by which doubt, or incertitude is dealt with during the decision task. If decision makers are uncertain as to the potential effectiveness or the results of a decision, they conform to the pre–established standard. This conformity should not be construed to mean that the decision will not have a solid foundation. In this case, conformity merely relates to the fact that the reasoning for the decision is based upon pre–determined guidelines.

An example of a scenario involving the process model of decision making is promoting a Marketing Representative of a company to a higher level. A group comprised of the Marketing Manager, HR Manager, and Compensation and Benefits Manager meet to discuss the promotion. Since the Marketing Manager has seen exemplary work from the representative, the Marketing Manager adamantly wants to promote the individual from a Marketing Representative I to a Marketing Representative III. In their negotiation, the HR Manager and Compensation and Benefits Manager point out to the Marketing Manager that company policy mandates that an employee can only be promoted one level at a time. Additionally, no precedent has been set to justify deviation from this policy. Therefore, the Marketing Representative is promoted to Marketing Representative II.

The Garbage Can Model

The fourth model of decision making is the garbage can model. This model is most appropriate for judgment tasks in organisations where the technologies are not clear, the involvement of participants fluctuates in the amount of time and effort given, and choices are inconsistent and not well defined.

In such an organisation, an opportunity to make a decision is described as a garbage can into which many types of problems and solutions are dropped independently of each other by decision–makers, as these problems and solutions are generated. The problems, solutions and decision makers are not necessarily related to each other. They move from one decision opportunity to another in such a manner that the solutions, the time needed and the problems seem to rely on a chance alignment of components to complete the decision. These components are the combination of options available at a given time, the combination of problems, the combination of solutions needing problems, and the external demands on the decision makers.

An example of the garbage can model is a company department trying to deplete its budget before the end of the fiscal year. This department, consisting of five employees, has additional money in its budget to use up by the end of the fiscal year. The employees do not want to lose the money. So, they create a bogus allocation in order to protect it, but really have no use for it. Two weeks after the end of the fiscal year, the department's computer system goes down. Fortunately, the solution (the money from the budget to replace the computer system), the problem (inoperable computer system) and the individuals involved (the employees) are in alignment. In other words, the timing is perfect for the combination of components to solve this problem: The employees protected budget money which could be used at a later time, the computer system went down, and the protected money could be used to buy a new computer system.

The notable advantage of the garbage can model is that it provides a real–world representation of the non–rational manner in which decisions are often made within an organisation. Not all decisions are made in a logical, political, or even standard fashion. Occasionally, decisions are made on an ad hoc basis or by 'flying by the seat of the pants' when the solutions, problems and individuals involved in the task happens to align.

Despite its representation of the non–rational, real–world manner in which decisions are often made, the garbage can model does have an important disadvantage. It is not the most efficient means of making a decision. Decision making is considered a procedure for finding solutions to problems. Unfortunately, this often does not happen if the garbage can model represents the manner in which decisions are made within an organisation. Problems are worked on in given situations, but choices are made only when the combination of problems, solutions and individuals allow the decision to happen (i.e., are in alignment). Consequently, the alignment of the problems, solutions, and individuals often occurs after the opportunity to make a decision regarding a problem has passed or occurs even before the problem has been discovered.

In discussing the four general models, the issue is not necessarily which model is the best one, because they all have advantages and disadvantages which may work or be appropriate for certain groups and situations. The purpose of using models to assess group decision making is to provide a base for comparison. A model is a starting point for evaluating a process, and group decision making is a process.

One way of evaluating this process is to determine which model, if any, a group is using to make decisions. The decision procedure can be analysed in order to facilitate the improvement of the procedure once the model is determined. The procedure can be improved by anticipating potential problems and acting accordingly.

For instance, time wasted due to a lack of direction and organisation can be eliminated. Knowing that a group makes decisions by following a rational model enables the decision makers to expedite the decision process. These individuals can expedite the process by preparing themselves for group meetings by becoming familiar with any goals or objectives, possible alternatives and consequences of these alternatives as well as potential optimal choices as they relate to a decision.

The knowledge that a group follows a political model in making decisions is also helpful. This knowledge can assist group members in preparing the supporting information for their perspective. This preparation can assist the individuals in presenting their viewpoint more persuasively. Consequently, their viewpoint has a better chance of being adopted as the one of choice.

Knowing that a group utilises a process model for making decisions can also increase the effectiveness of the decision procedure. Being aware that judgments are made relative to standard operating procedures enables individuals to anticipate potential obstacles to a decision. Consequently, these individuals can research the pre–established guidelines that may pose these problems and adjust their argument or point of view accordingly.

If group members are aware that decisions are made by using a garbage can model, they at least have the comfort of knowing that these decisions follow some sort of method. Granted the method is somewhat random and chaotic, but it should be kept in mind that it is a method nonetheless.

Moreover, identifying the model when the decision process does not function effectively is of value, because the decision makers then know the method to avoid. They should avoid the current model that produced the ineffective results. This avoidance can be accomplished by agreeing as a group to try to adopt a different approach (i.e. a new model).

It should be pointed out that even if the group decision–making procedure does not fit one of the aforementioned general models, the process of analysing the decision task in and of itself in order to identify a model is beneficial. This analysis provides valuable insight into the dynamics of how decisions are made within the group whether or not one of the four models is actually discovered. The cognitive flow of the group is important to note, because it enables an understanding of the other group members' rationale for judgment. Furthermore, this cognitive flow may spawn the creation of a novel group decision–making model.

In conclusion, models of group decision making can be helpful. They are not cure–alls for faulty decision procedures. They are merely a starting point for potential improvement. Models aid in assessing the interaction of group members regarding a judgment procedure. Group decision making models provide form to an intangible and abstract concept. Models promote the discovery and resolution of problems that can occur during the decision–making process.

CHAPTER 10

Rules for Taking Decisions

There are three major parameters for making a decision.

Majority Rule

- The quality of the group's decision is a particularly troublesome problem with majority rule.
- When decisions are not very important, decisions must be made quickly, and when commitment of all members to the final decision is unimportant, majority rule can be useful.
- Consensus becomes increasingly difficult the larger the group becomes

Minority Rule

- This occurs when the group designates an expert to make the decisions.
- A designated authority makes the decision for the group.
- Executive committees must be delegated responsibility for making certain decisions because the workload for the group as a whole is overwhelming or the time constrains are prohibitive.

Unanimity Rule (Consensus)

- Consensus is a state of mutual agreement among members of a group where all legitimate concerns of individuals have been addresses to the satisfaction of the group.

- Not all unanimous decisions can be considered a true consensus.
- True consensus requires agreement, commitment, and satisfaction
- Groups that use a consensus approach tend to produce better decisions than groups using other decision rules because full discussion of issues is requires, every group member must be convinced that the decision is a good one, and minority members will be heard.
- Members feel more confident about the correctness of their decisions with consensus and they are more satisfied with the group as a whole.
- Use a 'stand aside'– a team member continues to have reservations about the group decision, but when confronted does not want to block the group.
- Avoid conflict like, suppressing techniques such as coin–flipping and swapping (I'll support your position this time if you'll support mine next time).

More About Consensus Decision Making

Consensus refers to agreement on some decision by all members of a group, rather than a majority or a select group of representatives. The consensus process is what a group goes through to reach this agreement. The assumptions, methods, and results are very different from traditional parliamentary procedure or majority voting methods.

Consensus is based on the belief that each person has some part of the truth and that no one has all of it (no matter how tempting it is to believe that we ourselves *really* know best!) It is also based on a respect for all persons involved in the decision being considered.

Acting according to consensus guidelines enables a group to take advantage of all group members' ideas. By combining their

Rules	Pros	Con
Majority Rule	Quick Efficient Expedient in large groups	Minorities vulnerable to tyranny of majority Quality of decision suspect Usually alienate minority Under utilisation of resources
Minority Rule Designated Expert Designated Authority Executive Committee Forceful Faction	Saves time Clear, Efficient Divides Labour Faction may be informed/committed	Expertise hard to determine No group input Members vie for attention Members vie to impress authority Weak commitment to decision Likely we-not me oriented
Unanimity rule Consensus	Quality decisions Commitment Satisfaction	Time consuming Difficult Tension Producing

thoughts, people can often create a higher–quality decision than a vote decision or a decision by a single individual. Further, consensus decisions can be better than vote decisions because voting can actively undermine the decision. People are more likely to implement decisions they accept, and consensus makes acceptance more likely.

Requirements of Consensus Process

Consensus demands a high level of trust among the members of the group. People need to believe that each member is a fair and reasonable person of integrity who has the organisation's best interests at heart. There are no perfect groups or perfect individuals, but for consensus to work the members must believe interests at heart. There are no perfect groups or perfect individuals, but for consensus to work the members must believe that everyone is honestly doing their best.

Another important element of the consensus process is a good facilitator. This person is responsible for seeing that everyone is heard, that all ideas are incorporated if they seem to be part of the truth, and that the final decision is agreed upon by all assembled. The facilitator is the servant of the group, not its leader. It is his/her job to draw out and focus the best thinking of the group, not to use his/her position to impose or elevate his/her own.

It's important that the facilitator never show signs of impatience or disfavour towards an idea or a member. Total objectivity may an unattainable ideal, but the facilitator should strive to remain as neutral as possible in the discussion.

If he/she can't manage this, then someone else should be facilitating. For this reason, many groups rotate the facilitator role on some kind of regular schedule, or choose a facilitator for each discussion depending on who is willing to forgo taking a more active part.

A good facilitator needs to be patient, intuitive, articulate, able to think on his/her feet, and have a sense of humour. He/she should always be on the lookout for things that are missing—a person who wants to speak but has been too shy, an idea that was badly articulated or dismissed too quickly but has potential, or anything happening on the nonverbal level that might be significant. The facilitator should periodically state and restate the ideas on the table, the elements that have been agreed on, and the questions still being decided. This allows everyone to see that progress is being made, and to focus on the work left to be done.

Guidelines for Consensus Decision-making

- Come to the discussion with an open mind. This doesn't mean not thinking about the issue beforehand, but it does mean being willing to consider any other perspectives and ideas that come up in the discussion.
- Listen to other people's ideas and try to understand their reasoning.
- Describe your reasoning briefly so other people can understand you. Avoid arguing for your own judgments and trying to make other people change their minds to agree with you.
- Avoid changing your mind only to reach agreement and avoid conflict. Do not go along with decisions until you have resolved any reservations that you consider important.
- View differences of opinion as helpful rather than harmful.
- Avoid conflict-reducing techniques such as majority vote. Stick with the process a little longer and see if you can't reach consensus after all.

Variations on Basic Consensus

No matter how well the discussion is carried forward, how good the facilitator and how much integrity and trust exist in the group, there sometimes comes a point where all are in agreement but one or two. At this point there are a few possible courses of action.

One is to ask if the individuals are willing to "step aside." This means that they do not agree with the decision but do not feel that it is wrong. They are willing to have the decision go forward, but do not want to take part in carrying it out.

Depending on the size and nature of the group, if more than one or two people want to step aside from a decision, the group should probably take another look at it. The facilitator might ask for a few minutes of silence to see if there is another decision or an amendment that should have been considered but has been overlooked, or something that would ease the situation.

Another possibility is to lay aside the issue for another time. Although this alternative may create some difficulties, the world will probably continue to turn with or without a decision being made right now. The need to make a decision promptly is often not as important as the need to ultimately come to unity around a decision that has been well–crafted, taking the time it needs to do it right.

A third possibility is that one or two people may stop the group from moving forward. At this time there are several key considerations. Most important, the group should see those who are withholding consensus as doing so out of their highest understanding and beliefs.

Next, the individuals who are preventing the group from making the decision should also examine themselves closely to assure that they are not withholding consensus out of self–interest, bias, vengeance, or any other such feeling.

A refusal to enter consensus should be based on a very strong belief that the decision is wrong — and that the dissenters would be doing the group a great disservice by allowing the decision to go forward.

This is always one of those times when feelings can run high, and it's important for the group not to put pressure on those who differ. It's hard enough to feel that you are stopping the group from going forward, without feeling coerced to go against your examined reasons and deeply felt understandings.

Some groups operate under a modified consensus approach called 'Consensus–Minus–One.' This means that it takes more than one dissenting member to block consensus.

One voice at odds with the rest is considered a workable way to go forward, but more than one is a sign that the decision should be re–thought. Consensus–Minus–One can be a reassuring arrangement for people who are new to the process of consensus decision–making, or in groups where members aren't well acquainted enough to have the level of trust needed to commit to achieving full consensus.

In practice, many groups have found that Consensus–Minus–One serves as a safety valve that rarely gets used. If even one member has strong reservations about a decision, it's often enough to keep the group searching for a better answer.

Some Difficulties with Consensus

- Achieving consensus can take considerably longer than a simple majority vote.
- People who don't actively try to find a decision that is acceptable to everyone (all–win) can dominate a group's discussion by trying to make everyone else go along with them (win–lose).
- A group can coerce or manipulate individuals into saying they accept a decision, even when they don't. That is groupthink, not true consensus.

Consensus vs. Groupthink

Consensus and groupthink are different. Groupthink occurs when everyone expresses agreement with a decision, but some people are just going along because they feel obligated to reach an agreement and avoid conflict.

Thus although there appears to be a consensus, some people

have not resolved disagreements they consider important. In consensus, all agree with the decision and all important disagreements are resolved.

The time required to reach consensus can't usually be avoided. Instead, look at it as an investment in better decisions and a healthier, more egalitarian, more participatory organisation.

The other pitfalls can best be dealt with through openness and continuous effort on everyone's part to do what is ethical and right for the group. A willingness to take risks and to give and receive honest feedback is key to developing the trust required to let the process work.

CHAPTER 11

Facing Group Discussions

Whether you are participating in a group as a member or are directing the discussion as a leader, you need to have certain skills to make the discussion a success and yourself a winner.

Communication Skills

The first aspect is one's power of expression. In a GD, a candidate has to talk effectively so that he is able to convince others. For convincing, one has to speak forcefully and at the same time create an impact by his knowledge on the subject. A candidate who is successful in holding the attention of the audience creates a positive impact.

It is necessary that you should be precise and clear. As a rule evaluators do not look for the wordage produced. Your knowledge on a given subject, your precision and clarity of thought are the things that are evaluated. Irrelevant talks lead you nowhere. You should speak as much as necessary, neither more nor less. GDs are not debating stages.

Evaluators also judge the ability to listen. They look for your ability to react on what other participants say. Hence, it is necessary that you listen carefully to others and then react or proceed to add some more points. Your behaviour in the group is also put to test, i.e. how you interact with fellow participants. Whether you are a loner or can work in a group.

You should be able to convey your thoughts satisfactorily and convincingly before a group of people. Confidence and level headedness in doing so is necessary. These add value to your presentation. In case you are not good at it, you might gain by joining an institute that offers specialised courses in public speaking. For instance, many languages institutes offer a wide range of courses like conversation skills, business communication skills, business writing, negotiation skills and presentation skills. Mostly people attend these courses to improve their communication skills. Students here are involved in activities which use communication skills and teachers provide inputs, monitor and facilitate the classes. These courses make you confident enough to speak before people without any nervousness.

Knowledge and Ideas about a Subject

Knowledge of the subject under discussion and clarity of ideas are important. Knowledge comes from consistent reading on various topics ranging from science and technology to politics. In–depth knowledge makes one confident and enthusiastic and this in turn, makes one sound convincing and confident.

Leadership and Coordinating Capabilities

The basic aim of a group discussion is to judge a candidate's leadership qualities. The examiner withdraws and becomes a silent spectator once the discussion starts. A candidate should display tactfulness, skill, understanding and knowledge on varied topics, enterprise, forcefulness and other leadership qualities to motivate and influence other candidates who may be almost equally competent.

Exchange of Thoughts

A GD is an exchange of thoughts and ideas among members of a group. These discussions are held for selecting personnel in organisations where there is a high level of competition. The number of participants in a group can vary between 8 and 15. Mostly a topic or a situation is given to group members who have to discuss it between 10 and 20 minutes.

The purpose is to get an idea about candidates in a short time and make assessments about their skills, which normally cannot be evaluated in an interview. These skills may be team membership, leadership skills, listening and articulation skills.

A note is made of your contributions to the discussion, comprehension of the main idea, the rapport you strike, patience, assertion, accommodation, amenability, etc. Body language and eye contact too are important points which are to be considered.

Addressing the Group as a Whole

While in the GD it is not necessary to address anyone by name. Even otherwise you may not know everyone's names. It is better to address the group as a whole.

Address the person farthest from you. If he can hear you everyone else too can. Needless to add, as for interview, attend the GD in formal dress. The language used should also be formal, not the language used in normal conversations. For instance, words and phrases like '*yar*', '*chalta hai*', 'CP', 'I dunno', etc. are out. This is not to say you should use a high sounding, pedantic language. Avoiding both, just use formal, plain and simple language. Hinglish, (mixture of Hindi and English) should be discarded.

Confidence and coolness while presenting your viewpoint are of help. See that you do not keep repeating a point. Do not use more words than necessary. Do not be superfluous. Try to be specific. Do not exaggerate.

Thorough Preparation

Start making preparations for interview and GDs right away, without waiting till the eleventh hour, this is, if and when called for them. Then the time left may not be adequate. It is important to concentrate on subject knowledge and general awareness. Hence, the prime need for thorough preparation. Remember, the competition is very tough. Only 460 candidates make it to the final list from 2.75 lakh civil service aspirants each year.

It may so happen that you are called for interviews and group discussions from three or four organisations but are not selected by any. The reason obviously lies in your not being well–prepared. If basic intelligence level and personality are not matched with thorough preparation you may be a victim of 'Apply, apply, no reply.' You should ask yourself what can you do for your employers, not what can they do for you.

Here is an account of Nitya from Gujarat which makes the point amply clear, "In spite of doing an MBA in Marketing, I have not landed myself into any decent job. A few of the places I got rejected apparently because of my casual approach or bad luck. I have even sent my resume to numerous placement agencies but there has been no response. It is becoming embarrassing to face the family members and the society. Moreover, it is deteriorating my health, and is leading to severe depression and frustration."

In a GD you may be given a topic and asked to express your views on it. Or in a case study GD, students have to read a case study and suggest ways of tackling the problem. For this you should have a good general knowledge, need to be abreast with current affairs, threfore you should regularly read newspapers and magazines. Your group behaviour and communication skills are on test, i.e. how you convince others and how clearly you are able to express your points of view? You should be articulate, generate ideas, not sound boring, should allow others to speak adopt a stand on a given subject. During the course of the GD this stand can even be changed, giving the impression that you are open to accommodate others' viewpoints.

Additional marks may be given for starting or concluding the discussion.

Personal Skills

Judges often look for initiative displayed by the candidate, his extent of self–confidence, his depth of knowledge, group and level of understanding of the subject. Another important criterion would be the candidate's consistency in thinking and presentation of facts. The candidate must have his facts right. It is very important to see whether the candidate reiterates erroneous facts, whether he bombards others with data and confuses the issues at hand, whether he shows shallow understanding and superficial knowledge, etc. Such negative features if observed carefully, may make the task or rejection easier.

While selecting the right candidate, the ability in coherent organisation and logical development of thought is looked for. Equally important would be his personal skill of logical and rational reasoning. Again, it would be useful to see whether he is relaxed, pleasant, courteous and co–operative (not cold and aloof.) Moreover, it is extremely important to look for the vital skill of assertiveness (not aggressiveness) in the right candidates.

Group Skills

Judges also look for the candidate's extent of value addition to the group, his ability to communicate ideas fluently and efficiently, his ability to listen attentively as well as his willingness to listen to logic and reason, besides his ability for sustained interest. Again, the panel members focus their attention on the candidate's ability to enhance the quality of discussion; especially, his ability to contribute original points (not repeating the same points). Another major group skill would be the candidate's ability to discuss different dimensions. His ability to steer the group into discussing other angles is also looked for. Furthermore, it is observed whether the candidate has the ability to make consistent efforts to relate with others in the group. Last, but not the least is the candidate's ability to build on valid points.

Leadership Skill

In this category, the candidate's ability to influence and persuade others, his ability to encourage and also to compromise is looked for. Observe his ability to co–ordinate and summarise. Another important aspect would be his ability to build up the confidence of the group. It would be useful to look for his ability to encourage silent members into discussion.

Quick Look at Essential Qualities

The GD coordinator does the assessment of candidate's performance. Normally there are three GD coordinators and they sit in three different positions, each observing the group and noting down the relevant aspects. The coordinators and very senior people who have ample experience in man–management and hence they are easily able to examine the candidates. Following are the qualities that are looked for during a GD:

- **Leadership ability.** This is judged by:
  - Drive, initiative and enterprise.
  - Ability to give direction.
  - Shouldering responsibility.
  - Positive intervention and coordination.
  - Objectivity and goal fulfilment.
- **Knowledge.** No matter how much a candidate boasts of

his knowledge level. The judges come to their decision based on certain parameters, which include:

- Grasp of the subject matter.
- Value addition.
- Originality.
- Range of ideas.
- **Analytical ability.** The judges look for use of arguments, example and logic — how effectively are the same related to the subject matter.
- **Communication.** The ability to communicate of a candidate is judged by his:
- Fluency and clarity of thought.
- Presentation.
- Listening to others.
- Concise and clear–cut viewpoints.
- Conviction.
- Body language.
- **Group behaviour.** Here, judges look for:
- Persuasive ability.
- To carry peers along.
- To be able to get along with the group.

The panel may also assess you in terms of negative attributes like extremism in views, use of foul and abusive language, not following the instructions, aggressive body language, etc.

Chapter 12

Behavioural Traits and Discussion Etiquette

Behaviour is something, which is as important in a GD as what you say, as it gives a sketch of your personality. Behave in a GD, as you would like to behave in a boardroom, in an assertive, friendly and dignified manner.

Shouting – A BIG NO

A GD is not a throat-cleaning exercise and your decibel levels would take you nowhere. So, you must not shout. There may be and there will be cases when the whole group starts shouting and chaos is created. In such a case, if you too start shouting, you will be seen to be as bad as your whole group. Whatever you say will anyway be drowned as nobody would be able to hear it properly. In such a scenario, try to divert the group from the point of discussion which was the cause of chaos and start some new sub – topic. Or if you can, put some new ideas so that the group jumps on to it and sanity is restored. It is understandable that all this is easier said than done. But then, winning never comes easy!

Display an Open Mind

As mentioned earlier, GD is not about fighting for your stand. Stick to your ideas if you are convinced but do not rubbish others. Just a word of appreciation for any decent idea (even if it comes from your opposition) or just a phrase to say that the other side too can be thought about will go a long way in making you acceptable to the whole group and much more importantly, to the panel.

Mind your Posture and Body Movement

Your posture conveys a lot of information about your attitude. Too much laid back posture with all your weight on your back gives the impression of you being a non–committed and non–involved person. On the other hand, too much of forward bend makes you a shaky person. Try to look at the person who is speaking (if that's not you!) and try to address the whole group while speaking. Don't make it a corner discussion. Your hand movements are one thing that gets noticed pretty fast. Exaggerated hand movement denotes that you are facing problems communicating your ideas in words. So that's not advisable. But if you have hand movements, don't curb them too much. That way, your normal body language would get affected.

Remember, a GD is all about remaining normal in an abnormal scenario. And whatever good things you do, it's important that you are seen doing all that by the panel members! So now, get set and get cracking!!

Avoid these GD Mistakes at all Costs

Emotional Outburst

Hema was offended when one of the male participants in a group discussion made a statement on women generally being submissive while explaining his point of view. When Hema finally got an opportunity to speak, instead of focussing on the topic, she vented her anger by accusing the other candidate for being a male chauvinist and went on to defend women in general.

What Hema essentially did was to:

- Deviate from the subject.
- Treat the discussion as a forum to air her own views.
- Lose objectivity and make personal attacks.

Her behaviour would have been perceived as immature and de–motivating to the rest of the team.

Quality Vs. Quantity

Jatin believed that the more he talked, the more likely he was to get through the GD. So, he interrupted other people at every opportunity. He did this so often that the other candidates got together to prevent him from participating in the rest of the discussion.

Remember:

- Assessment is not only on your communication skills but also on your ability to be a team player.
- Evaluation is based on quality, and not on quantity. Your contribution must be relevant.
- The mantra is 'Contributing meaningfully to the team's success.' Domination is frowned upon.

Egotism Showing off

Phagun was happy to have got a group discussion topic he had prepared for. So, he took pains to project his vast knowledge of the topic with views like:

"Every other sentence of his contained statistical data – '20% of companies"; "24.27% of parliamentarians felt that; I recently read in a Jupiter"; "Report that..." and so on so forth. Soon, the rest of the team either laughed at him or ignored his attempts to enlighten them as they perceived that he was cooking up the data.

So, take care of these points:

- Exercise restraint in anything. You will end up being frowned upon if you attempt showing–off your knowledge.
- Facts and figures need not validate all your statements.
- It's your analysis and interpretation that are equally important – not just facts and figures.
- You might be appreciated for your in–depth knowledge. But you will fail miserably in your people skills.

Such a behaviour indicates how self–centered you are and highlights your inability to work in an atmosphere where different opinions are expressed.

Get Noticed – But for the Right Reasons

Kumar knew that everyone would compete to initiate the discussion. So as soon as the topic – 'Discuss the negative effects of India joining the WTO' – was read out, he began talking. In his anxiety to be the first to start speaking, he did not hear the word 'negative' in the topic. He began discussing the ways in which the country had benefited by joining WTO, only to be stopped by the evaluator, who then corrected his mistake.

Remember that:

- False starts are extremely expensive. They cost you your admission. It is very important to listen and understand the topic before you air your opinions.
- Spending a little time analysing the topic may provide you with insights which others may not have thought about. Use a pen and paper to jot down your ideas.
- Listen! It gives you the time to conceptualize and present the information in a better manner.

- Some mistakes are irreparable. Starting off the group discussion with a mistake is one such mistake, unless you have a great sense of humour.

Manage your Insecurities

Radhika was very nervous. She thought that some of the other candidates were exceptionally good. Thanks to her insecurity, she contributed little to the discussion. Even when she was asked to comment on a particular point, she preferred to remain silent.

- Your personality is also being evaluated. Your verbal and non verbal cues are being read.
- Remember, you are the participant in the GD; not the evaluator. So, rather than evaluating others and your performance, participate in the discussion.
- Your confidence level is being evaluated. Decent communication skills with good confidence is a must to crack GDs.
- Focus on your strengths and do not spend too much time thinking about how others are superior or inferior to you. It is easy to pick up these cues from your body language.

Always Remember

Knowledge is strength. A candidate with good reading habits has more chances of success. In other words, sound knowledge on different topics like politics, finance, economy, science and technology is helpful.

Power to convince effectively is another quality that makes you stand out among others. Clarity in speech and expression is yet another essential quality. If you are not sure about the topic of discussion, it is better not to initiate. Lack of knowledge or wrong approach creates a bad impression. Instead, you might adopt the wait and watch attitude. Listen attentively to others, may be you would be able to come up with a point or two later.

A GD is a formal occasion where slangs are to be avoided. A GD is not a debating stage. Participants should confine themselves to expressing their viewpoints. In the second part of the discussion, candidates can exercise their choice in agreeing, disagreeing or remaining neutral.

Language used should be simple, direct and straight forward.

Don't interrupt a speaker when the session is on. Try to score by increasing your size, not by cutting others short.

Maintain rapport with fellow participants. Eye contact plays a major role. Non–verbal gestures, such as listening intently or nodding while appreciating someone's viewpoint speak of you positively.

Communicate with each and every candidate present. While speaking, don't keep looking at a single member. Address the entire group in such a way that everyone feels you are speaking to him or her.

Things to Do During a GD

- Speak pleasantly and politely to the group.
- Respect the contribution of all speakers.
- Remember that a discussion is not an argument. Learn to disagree politely.
- Think about your contribution before you speak. Consider how best can you answer the question/contribute to the topic.
- Try to stick to the discussion topic. Don't introduce irrelevant information.

- Be aware of your body language when you are speaking.
- Agree with and acknowledge what you find interesting.

Things Not to Do during a GD

- Lose your temper. A discussion is not an argument.
- Shout. Use a moderate tone and medium pitch.
- Use too many gestures when you speak.
- Gestures like finger pointing and table thumping can appear aggressive.
- Dominate the discussion. Confident speakers should allow quieter students a chance to contribute.
- Draw too much on personal experience or anecdote. Although some encourage students to reflect on their own experience, remember not to generalise too much.
- Interrupt. Wait for a speaker to finish what they are saying before you speak.

Destructive Roles and Behaviours to Avoid

- Denial and equivocation
- Changing topics
- Noncommittal remarks
- Irreverent joking
- Remarks with contempt
- Name calling
- Hostile humour
- Mockery sarcasm
- Confrontative remarks through gestures e.g. sneering, rolling eyes, curling upper lip
- Criticism with personal attacks
- Criticism by blaming
- Defensiveness through denial of responsibility

- Making excuses
- Negative mind–reading
- Cross–complaining
- Trading blame
- Defensiveness by saying, 'yes...but...'
- Repeating self
- Whining
- Stone walling
- Defensiveness through body language, like crossing arms, etc.

CHAPTER 13

Speaking Skills in a Group Discussion

As a participant in a GD, the skills involved in getting your point across are not vastly different than those of a keynote speaker giving a speech to a group.

According to a renowned speech coach and communications authority, "Just because the spotlight isn't shining directly on you doesn't mean that you can't be seen."

Like public speaking, the art of effective business–meeting communication is very much a learnable skill. Here are eight important, yet often overlooked tips on speaking well as a meeting participant.

Keep it upbeat. Speech tips and body language aside, nothing is more critical to constructive give–and–take in a meeting than emphasising the upside. Rather than criticising, stay focussed on the implicit value of what someone else says. A comprehensive study suggests that a preponderance of positive remarks at business meetings genuinely contributes to successful companies. Try keeping score between positive comments and those designed more to sting than support. "Stay solution focussed, offering up twice as many positive comments as you do negative," an expert says. "When it's possible, affirm others' ideas by using active and constructive feedback. For example, "I really like Bill's idea on how we can use a different approach when responding to customer complaints."

Talk to the entire group. We've all been treated like a fifth wheel — being part of a group, but somehow off the planet when someone is supposedly addressing everyone in the room. Don't make the same mistake. When speaking in a group move your eyes around and talk to anyone who's listening to what you have to say. "When responding to a question, address the entire group, not just the person who asked the question," an expert says. "In this way, everyone feels included."

Reach out and encourage feedback. Another meeting pitfall is that hollow sound of silence — comments by speakers that disappear over the horizon leaving no follow–up discussion in their wake. This silence is not golden. So actively encourage comment and feedback based on what you have to contribute. Not only does that make for a better meeting, but it can broaden, amplify and substantiate your remarks.

"Get your point across but also open it up for discussion," says a consultant. "Call on people and ask them what they think. The point is not just to be a participant, but also a facilitator."

Mirror the tenor of the meeting. Another group speaking basic is establishing a comfortable atmosphere where everyone feels at ease. One effective way to achieve that is to establish a consistency in communication. If, for instance, most participants are keeping their remarks short, do the same. If their tone is low and reserved, follow their lead.

The point is not to mindlessly mimic but, rather, to affirm and contribute to the overall tenor of the meeting. And that makes for productive and efficient give and take. "You can also mirror other behaviours such as leaning forward, crossing your legs and other movements," another expert says.

Don't be a time hog. Anyone speaking in a group wants to take enough time to identify and, if need be, dissect the point he's trying to convey. But it's all too easy to slip into a filibuster.

Experts identify this element as conversational balance. Be thorough, but don't take so much time to get your message across that you lose others' attention or, even worse, alienate someone who may be waiting his turn to talk. Again, if others are being succinct, try to do the same. If need be, keep an eye on your watch when you've got the floor so a comment meant to be short doesn't dissolve into a diatribe.

Check the clichés and rhetoric. A central tenet of powerful group communication is being as clear as possible. Don't muddy your message by wallowing in tired catch phrases — just watch for facial tics when you suggest 'pushing the envelope' — or too many rhetorical questions that don't advance the discussion. "Be particularly careful with negative rhetorical remarks like, 'What were you thinking?" says an expert.

When and if necessary, take it offline. Not every in–meeting topic warrants brain surgery. Don't derail meetings or drag them on endlessly by going into detail that can be addressed at another time. If you make a point that warrants a lot more discussion, tell someone that you'll talk about it in greater detail at some other time. Or address the issue one–on–one with the questioner after the meeting.

Be aware of your body. Not everything you convey to others comes by way of your mouth. How you say what you say is equally telling in your ability to share your thoughts with others.

Vocabulary for Debates and Discussion

When you want to state an opinion:

Informal

- In my opinion____
- I think that_____
- I feel that_____

- I believe that______
- It seems to me that________
- If you ask me______
- I'd say that_______
- The point is________
- As I see it_______
- I'd say that______
- The point is______

Formal

- You know what I think... I think that____
- Wouldn't you say that_______?
- Don't you agree that_______?
- I'd just like to say that______
- I'd like to point out that_______

When you want someone to repeat or explain

- I don't understand what you mean
- Would you explain that, please?
- I'm sorry, but I didn't understand your point.
- Could you give an example?
- What do you mean by_____?

When you want to agree with someone (in ascending order of formality)

- You're right
- I think so, too
- I agree with you
- You could be right
- I couldn't agree more
- That's a good point

- I couldn't agree more
- I see what you mean
- That's just what I was thinking
- I agree entirely
- You know, that's exactly what I think

When you want to disagree with someone (in ascending order of formality)

- Yes, but_____
- I disagree
- That's not the point
- No, I think you're wrong
- Up to a point, but________
- Yes, that's quite true, but_____
- I'm not sure I quite agree
- Well, you have a point there, but_____
- Perhaps, but don't you think that_____
- I see what you mean, but________
- I tend to disagree with you there

Informal disagreement (between people you know very well)

- I can't agree with you there!
- You can't be serious!!
- Come off it!
- Don't be silly!

When you want to persuade someone:

- You must admit that___
- Do you really believe that_____?
- Don't you think that______?
- Don't you agree that____?

Chapter 14

Body Language

Never underestimate the importance of body language during a job interview. Make sure you're sending all the right messages to the people who are watching you. Remember that saying 'A picture is worth a thousand words'? Turns out it isn't just about photographs and essays. 'People believe what they see over what they hear,' explains an expert. Facial expressions and gestures account for 55% of meaning.

How we come across to someone is decided only for a small part by the words we speak. To leave a good impression behind, say at a job interview, it is important that we know, and to a certain extent can control, our body language. The person on the receiving end of our body language will have a feeling or impression that is often difficult to describe – difficult to put into words or difficult to prove what actually was communicated. Haven't we all said at times, 'I have a feeling he/she likes me', or something like: 'I doubt if what he/she is saying is really the truth'.

This type of feeling is called intuition. Body language plays a big role in intuition as it gives us messages about the other person that we can interpret at an intuitive level. It is, therefore, necessary to get to know our own body language first. We should learn about it so that we can recognise it in others as well as in ourselves.

Everyone uses Body Language

People can not live without each other, we are social beings. As soon as we are in contact with others we are communicating. For this we can make use of spoken and written language. In these ways we make the content of a message clear to each other. However we can also communicate without words. This kind of communication tells us something about the relationship between people. Often this is more important than getting the content of the message across. The communication about this non spoken communication, which tells us something about the relationship between people, is called Meta–Communication. Communicating about communication!

Words are Not Enough

When we connect with a person, we also have to make it clear to each other how the content of a spoken message needs to be interpreted. How we do this says something about the relationship we have with the other person, or think we have anyway. Often words are inadequate for this purpose. For instance we do not tell each other that easily how we feel about each other, or how the words of a message need to be interpreted. To make the meaning of our words clear we use body language. Body language is a language without spoken words and is therefore called non verbal communication. We use body language all the time, for instance looking someone in the eyes means something different than not looking someone in the eyes. In contact with others it is just not possible to be not communicating something.

Body Language Occurs Unconsciously

Yet the body language we use decides to a large extent the quality of our communication. It follows that therefore it would be good to become conscious of our own and others' body language. We can learn to use our body language for a purpose. As well as learn to understand and interpret body language of others. It is important to note that body language has different meanings in different cultures. How we can interpret body language depends on the situation, the culture, the relationship we have with the person as well as the gender of the other. This means that there is not one signal that has the same meaning all over the world. If you do not take this into account you may get yourself in some serious trouble! Body language is also interlinked with spoken language and a whole pattern of behaviour from a person. As well as that, various body language signs can complement each other to make a particular meaning crystal clear or strengthen the meaning of what we communicate. Some groups have developed a whole specific body language which can be very explicit in its meaning and is used to communicate where the use of words may otherwise be difficult or dangerous. Examples of this are mostly groups, such as gay people, people in slavery, prisoners, etc. who have a history of prejudice against them from the dominant culture.

Expression of Feelings

Body language is used especially to express feelings. For instance if we do not like someone, it is often difficult to say that directly to the person. However we can make it clear either intentionally or unintentionally through body language. The opposite is also true. We may say that we are angry through words yet our body language may be saying loud and clear that we are not. This can be very confusing for the receiver. This is usually described as giving out double messages – one message in words and an opposite message in body language. It is also difficult to lie or cover up our feelings through body language. People may give their true feelings away by not being aware of their body language. Research has shown that most people pay more attention to, and believe more readily, their impression of how a person acts through body language than what is said through words. As a consequence we tend to doubt, or put a question mark behind, the spoken words if they do not correspond with the language of the body.

Body Language as Part of Communication

Body language is definitely revealing, but at the same time should not be seen separately from all other forms of communication.

Contact and Interaction

When you look up the word communication on the Internet with the help of a search engine, you will get a screen filled with referrals to web sites about computers and telephony. We have almost forgotten what communication is all about – contact and interaction between people. Of course a telephone, a computer or a fax can be used for this. This usually concerns communication over a long distance, but it can also concern contact with a colleague in the next room.

Usually we do not use any tools when communicating over a short distance, meaning when we are in direct contact with someone. Then, we communicate through speech and body language. In the communication theory the same terms are used for describing all forms of communication, whether that is with tools or without.

Message, Sender and Receiver

When one or more people communicate, information is transmitted. In the communication theory this information is called the message. The person who transmits a message to the other person is called the sender, and the person who receives the message is called the receiver. With communication there is two–way traffic. This means that the receiver is a sender as well, because the receiver always reacts on the sender. A notable author opines that it is impossible not to communicate. Even when you say nothing at all, you still show something through your body language. It makes a big difference if you look at the other person or not, or if you are close or far away. Even your absent–mindedness, your silence, or your forthcoming answer conveys a message to the other person. Communication can take place consciously as well as subconsciously.

Interpreting Information

When two people are sitting together in a living room, and one is reading a book while the other is watching television, there is still communication between them. However we usually don't regard this as communication. In daily life when we speak about communication, we usually mean the conscious transfer of information. By this we mean that the message that the sender (consciously) transfers to the receiver will also be understood by the receiver. In order to be best able to transfer the information that the sender wants transmitted to the receiver, the sender will have to put himself in the receiver's shoes (level of understanding, emotional condition, previous experiences and the like). This is called the image formation phase. This still concerns the sender's thoughts.

Reading minds is not a gift that many people have. So when a person wants to transfer his thoughts to another person, he first has to translate them into something that is understandable to the other person. This translation of thoughts into words is called 'encoding' in the communication theory. When you translate these words back into thoughts, you are decoding. When people are talking to each other, the sender encodes his message in spoken language and the receiver then decodes those words. After the receiver has decoded the message he will try to interpret the information. The central question here is. 'What does this mean to me?'

Channels of Communication

We always choose some method for transferring the message. This can take place for example through writing, words or gestures. The medium that is used when transmitting the message is called the channel. There are sensory channels such as eyesight, hearing, feelings, smell and taste, mechanical channels such as pen or typewriter and electronic channels such as radio, telephone and computer.

Frame of Reference

Whether the message comes across or not to the other person depends on different factors. It is important for example that the sender knows, or assumes something, about the history and the background of the receiver. For example, if one was on vocation in England it would be quite naive to ask directions in Dutch. The chance of the other person understanding him is quite slim. But the body language codes also differ between cultures. Desmond Morris describes in 'The Naked Ape' a tragic incident whereby people from another culture interpreted a simple hand gesture meaning 'come here' in the wrong way. Northern Europeans signal in a different manner than Southern Europeans. In the North they signal with the palm of the hand upwards and in the South this is done with the palm downwards. The another gives an example of two Northern European men who were swimming in the sea and misinterpreted the hand gesture of several armed militaries. The militaries gestured that they had to come out of the water while they thought that they had to leave. The militaries shot them because they thought they were spies. This is a tragic example of miscommunication through a different frame of reference.

Noise

In communication between people, many things can go wrong. When someone tells you something in a noisy discotheque, there is a big chance that you will miss parts of the story. When someone invites you to take a seat, with a hand gesture, you will probably miss this message if it causes him to drop a tray with teacups. The external factors that distract the receiver, and therefore disrupt the communication, are called external noise. For example, a stuffy and sweaty lecture room can flag the attention of students. The right thing for the teacher to do is to limit the noise as much as possible in his transfer, in this case by opening a window. Noise can also occur because there is something wrong with the channels of communication, for example a disturbance in one of the senses, a cracking telephone line or the sender's handwriting being illegible. The correct understanding of the information transmitted can also be hindered by internal factors on the receiver's end. This is called internal noise. For example, the receiver can have incorrect expectations with regard to the message, be emotional, or not have enough prior knowledge of the subject. He can also be distracted by his own thoughts.

Feedback

For the sender of the message it is important to know if the message has arrived at the receiver in the manner he intended. He can find this out through a reaction from the receiver. When the receiver looks at him, and nods, he can assume that the receiver is listening. But in order to find out if the receiver has truly understood what he wanted to transmit, he could for example ask if the receiver wants to repeat the message in his own words. When a reaction is given to the message we speak about feedback. We can distinguish between verbal and non–verbal feedback. Non–verbal feedback is for example a frown, banging a fist on the table, or a deep sigh when hearing an unpleasant announcement. Because of this, the sender can be aware that his message has come across. Feedback can be given consciously as well as subconsciously.

Content and Relation

Through communicating with other people we can send messages on a content level and on a relational level. When you communicate on a content level it is about transmitting concrete substantive information. On a relational level it is about how a message should be interpreted, and how the relationship is between the people concerned. A message is often transmitted on a content level and on a relational level at the same time. For example, someone can say, 'Gosh, that dress must have cost a fortune!'

On a content level a comment is made about the price of the dress. On a relational level this sentence can have different meanings, for example:

- What a nice dress!
- You have paid way too much for that dress!
- You are way too easy with your money.
- I am jealous that you have so much money to spend.
- I would like to have a dress like that as well.
- That dress looks expensive, but I actually think it's really ugly.
- What a cheap rag!
- And you tell me that I spend a lot of money!

Three Aspects

Communication at a relational level consists of the following three aspects:

- The expressive aspect
- The relational aspect
- The appealing aspect

The *expressive aspect* says something about how the sender

expresses himself and the impression this makes on the receiver: Does he make a professional impression or is he a layman? Does he come across as reliable? Is he friendly or not? Does he have time, is he restless, or does he seem to be in a hurry? Does he act personal or distant? Is he insolent and arrogant or polite instead?

The *relational aspect* says something about how the receiver regards the relation with the sender: Is the position of the sender equal, higher or subordinate? Does the receiver rate the intelligence of the sender to be high or low? Is the receiver appreciative or disparaging in relation to the sender? Is the receiver interested or indifferent?

With the *appealing aspect* it is about how the content of the message is being transmitted by the receiver. The message can be transmitted in different ways: ordering, questioning, requesting, begging or informing.

Often the content of the message is expressed in words, and the relation with the help of body language. The intonation and the facial expression especially play a big part in this. Just say the aforementioned sentence about the dress in different intonations and you will find that it takes on different meanings. Non–verbal communication communicates about the verbal communication. When in doubt about the truth of the message or the sincerity of the speaker, people tend to believe non–verbal communication over verbal communication.

Metacommunication

Besides the content, it is good to also get the relational aspects of the communication clear. In order to achieve this, it is necessary to address the other person, or ask him questions, about his method of communicating. Like this, we do not speak about the content of the message, but about the meaning behind it and its relational aspect. So, in fact we communicate about the communication. This is called *metacommunication*, 'You say that it doesn't matter to you that our appointment is cancelled, but I can see in your face and hear from your voice that you are disappointed, aren't you?' Often the content of a message is represented in words and the relation is made clear by means of body language.

People can be surprised when you address them on the relational aspects of the communication, when for example you say something about their facial expression instead of about the content of their message. Still, metacommunication is very important within a relationship to get intentions and relations clear. However, some people actually know how to disturb the communication by metacommunicating at the wrong moments. When it should be about content, they give an answer on a relational level, and when they are addressed on their method of communicating they refer to the importance of the content. For example, when a colleague addresses them on errors in their work, they formulate an answer in which they describe the relation with their colleague, which is not so good. When the colleague then addresses them about their manner of communicating, they mention an example concerning the content but absolutely not related to the subject, for example about the way in which the colleague carries out his duties.

Non-verbal Communication

In the communication theory seven functions of the non-verbal communication are distinguished:

1. Repeating what has already been expressed verbally *(saying yes and nodding at the same time, giving directions and pointing)*.
2. Replacing the verbal communication *(nodding yes, shaking no, questioning facial expression, emblem gestures)*.

3. Opposing the verbal communication *(confirming something but shaking your head hesitantly or shrugging your shoulders)*.
4. Affectionate (instinctive) support of the spoken word *(concerned frown or encouraging pat on the back)*.
5. Information about the mutual relation *(smiling, eye contact, touching, distance, posture)*.
6. Emphasising the verbal communication *(a wagging finger when you express an accusation, or reproaching someone with a loud voice and hitting the table angrily)*.
7. Structuring and regulating the verbal communication *(the dots and commas of the spoken sentences: hemming, looking at someone and looking away, pauses, and supporting hand gestures)*.

Body Language and Daily Contacts

When we come in contact with other people, we always communicate. This can take place through using words, via our voice – spoken language – but also without, or alongside the use of words – non-spoken language or non–verbal communication. Posture and movements, our place in space, use of time and intonation when we speak are all part of this. Non–verbal communication is better known as body language. However, it is more than just body language.

The fact that body language is granted such a high reliability value might be due to the fact that a lot of non–verbal behaviour is hereditary or is taught to everyone in the same way at a very young age. It is ingrained so to speak.

We can express feelings of hate, fear, enjoyment, sadness and other primary human feelings to other people, without having to learn it. The understanding of emotions that are expressed via body language is probably also hereditary. This does not mean that we do not have to learn to recognise many gestures, which can mean one thing in one society and something else in another. Many body signals are not universal. In the most European countries and America for example, people shake their head when they mean no and nod when they mean yes, but there are cultures, for example in India or in Greece, where they mean the opposite – up and down means no and shaking means yes. The latter could be the evidence that this body language is taught rather than innate. In any case, the impressions that someone gives based on his body language are believed sooner than what he says about his feelings. Often people also give more attention to the non–verbal metacommunication than to the words of other people.

Communication Control is Important

How you come across, is not only determined by the words you speak. Communication control is important, for example to leave a good impression behind after a job interview. Hereby attention for your own body language is also important. Body language often just leaves an unclear feeling behind with the receiver. For example, 'I have the feeling that he likes me' or 'I doubt his sincerity'. It is not easy to express these feelings in words and the assumed meaning is not easy to prove. According to Oomkes the reason for this is the fact that digital and analogue languages are processed in the left and right side of the brain respectively. The right side of the brain deals with the more instinctive processes among other things, which are coupled with the recognition of total images (the analogue language). Therefores, the so–called intuitive recognition of another gesture, or behaviour pattern – the so-called subconscious understanding of the actions of another person – has nothing to do with a subject as unclear as intuition, according to Oomkes. Since the left side of the brain deals with the language of words and is less suitable for putting the images from the right side of the brain into words, it is very difficult for us to put in words the impressions of body behaviour of other people. Still we can learn to recognise and translate this non–verbal behaviour.

Intonation and Voice

A message can be added to the words we are using in a spoken sentence by using an intonation in our voice. This will let the receiver know what way the message needs to be interpreted.

For instance a question such as 'Why have you not told me this before now?' can be communicated in a variety of ways by using different intonations. In this way we can add expressions such as anger, disappointment or happiness to the actual words. When talking on the phone we can not make use of body signals like gestures, facial expression and touch. The receiver can not see our body language and therefore we often compensate for that by putting more emphasis on the way we use the intonations in our voice.

Ahs, Hums, Hesitations and Pauses

Our conversations are full of ahs, hums, hesitations and pauses. These guide our conversations and provide spaces for us to think and feel. They occur more when the subject is difficult or emotional or when we feel unsure of ourselves. If a public speaker addresses the audience for the first time, it will be noticeable that his/her speech gets more and more fluent as she/he speaks longer. This occurs only if there are no negative body language signals from the audience. This gives the speaker confidence, and by becoming more confident his/her speech will become more fluent. A good speaker pays attention to the body language signals from the audience and if possible adjusts the speech accordingly – or adjusts the way he/she delivers it.

Hearing Emotions in a Voice

It is possible to hear emotions in a voice. Our voice will tremble if we are feeling emotional and still need to/ want to continue talking. The tremble can indicate various emotions and can be interpreted differently by men and women, as well as by each individual. It is important to keep in mind that the situation, as well as gender and culture, can play a role in determining those differences. Some people use noisy actions such as clearing a throat or coughing when they find themselves in a tense situation. Spontaneous coughing and throat clearing occurs a lot more at official occasions when there is a request for silence! The whole range of emotions and ways to express them is not only closely related to the intonations in our voice and body language but also to our breathing. For example, think of when we sigh, laugh or cry.

Silence

Silences are another important aspect in communication. A whole web page could be written about the role of silences in our communication. When we are silent we are also communicating! What we communicate depends on what kind of silence it is. Mostly the subject of the conversation plays a major role in this. Again, the time in between words provide feeling and thinking space for people. Generally, the more emotionally loaded the subject is, the more silence we need. To *not talk*, to be silent in company when there is a lot of talking is an art in itself. Many people tend to think that when there is a silence there is just nothing more to say. Not true! It often means that people are trying to figure out something intuitively about themselves or the other(s). Quite often too they are noticing something about the body language of the other(s) and are paying attention to that.

Silence to be Intimate with Others

Sometimes people need silence to work out how intimate they want to be with others. Silences in group conversations are difficult to handle for a lot of people. They make them nervous, or they feel that they have to say something and can get embarrassed if they have nothing to add at that moment. It is at moments like these that we all say strange, stupid or boring things and later wonder why we did that – or worse, dislike ourselves for saying such stupid things! The weather, or other standard socially acceptable superficial conversation topics, is often used to fill up those gaps. It's always good to have a few standard comments up your sleeve in case of acute embarrassment. People who do not like to talk about a particular topic for whatever reason will use a silence or break in the conversation to create a distraction by changing topics. In the therapeutic world, silences are often used to give someone the opportunity to become more aware of themselves or what they have just said. If it is in a group, then silence can indicate a level of comfort and intimacy as well as distrust. Again, it depends on many other factors how the silence is interpreted. Silences can make some people feel threatened. Of course, when there is a silence it can be threatening, as everyone becomes more aware of his or her own body and their body language – especially if they have read this web site about it!

Posture

We can tell something about a person when we notice his or her body posture, the way people hold themselves gives important information. For instance, a lot of people feeling low will give that information by the way they hold their shoulders. Not only do we see it in their body posture, shoulders sagging and head down, but also in the way they have very little eye contact. They say to the world in fact that they are not interested in their environment nor the people in it. Compare that to someone who walks straight and looks at the world and immediately you will have another impression of how this person is feeling. Our body posture often reflects quite well how we feel. Try walking upright and looking around next time when you are feeling a bit low and you will notice that such a simple thing already influences your mood positively.

Interest and Respect

Another feeling we can communicate with our body posture is one of interest and respect for someone else. Turning your body to someone when they are talking to you indicates that you are interested in hearing what they have to say. It is an act of friendliness and respect and often rewards itself when you get it back from the other person. A small effort in this way can make the difference between being accepted by others or not.

Closed or Open

A body posture can be closed or open. Someone who does not feel too comfortable when they are with someone else will often assume a closed position. He or she will possibly have crossed arms or legs or will hold an object such as a bag in front. The bag as well as the crossed arms and legs provide a bit of a barrier and protection for feeling vulnerable. Trust has a lot to do with it and it is often natural to begin the contact with someone you do not know with a bit of a closed body position until you have established some level of trust and comfort that goes with that. Or in other words have established a level of intimacy. Intimacy can be anything from feeling good in the company of a person to being intimate physically. There are all sorts of levels of intimacy, also described as feelings of closeness. Remember, trust gets established by our body language interactions as well as what we say.

Movement

We are often not conscious of the kind of body language signals we send out, yet unconsciously we are able to interpret the body language of others. We rely on our intuitive feelings with this process of interpreting. Movement also belongs in body language. All movements, in our face, with our head, our legs, our feet and all body parts, our gestures, combine to make our body language congruent. Gestures, combinations of a series of smaller body movements, can be learned. Take, for instance, the gesture when we want to say *ok*: our thumb and index finger make a circle and our other fingers stretch upwards, while our facial expression compliments what we are signing with this signal. It is often funny how young children learn these signals and do not always get them right. It can also be funny, as well as cause difficulties, when a gesture means one thing in one culture and another thing in another culture. So, pay attention when and where you use them. These kinds of gestures have of course nothing to do with the learned sign language of deaf people, even though that language is made up out of series of gestures. Some of the principals of body language do not apply in the same way for deaf people when they are sign–talking.

Distance and space

'How we guard our personal space boundaries and how we enter into the others' personal space, is integrally connected with the way we are related with other people'.

It is important for people to have their 'own space'. The position someone prefers and all the things he does to appropriate the space around him says something about that person.

Is a visitor at a birthday party sitting between other people or does he sit somewhere separate? With whom is he sitting together? And is his place situated in the middle of a group or on the periphery? How much space between himself and others does this person create? Is he facing the door, the window or does he sit towards other people in the room?

Another aspect of space is the way people fit their home to make it a place of their own. If you watch someone's home on the inside, this tells you a lot about that person. How is the personal space divided? Are the rooms very full with material objects or empty? How much space (territory) do you think this person needs?

Distance during Interaction

The mutual distances people choose during interactions have several goals. Distance plays a role in signaling the beginning and the end of a conversation. It also signals something about how intimate and how personal we experience the relationship and the topic of discussion. The appropriate use of distance between talking partners is regulated by quite a lot of (unwritten) social rules and cultural norms.

Closeness

The physical distance we keep from others and our reaction to how other people approach us, have a big influence on our discussions and the accompanying connections with these people. The amount of personal space we appreciate is strongly influenced by our culture. This also counts for the mutual distance in which we feel confident during a business meeting.

If somebody comes closer to us than we are used to, invading our personal space, he can give us an uneasy feeling. We feel inclined to take a step backward to establish the original personal space with which we are comfortable again. In general, people need a certain amount of personal space to feel optimally o.k. This also indicates our wish to trace out our personal territory. When we are not at home we sometimes make a kind of temporary territory – a temporary space which we secure with our personal belongings. In this way we create a kind of personal air bubble around us. One who enters in there without being invited can count on a rejecting or angry response.

Zones

Edward Hall, an American anthropologist, has divided interpersonal space into four zones:

- The intimate zone (0 – 45 cm)
- The personal zone (45 – 120 cm)
- The social zone (120 – 360 cm)
- The public zone (360 – 750 cm or more)

Meeting Without the Use of Words

During a meeting people are communicating continuously, and not only the people who are speaking. Everybody who is present expresses non–verbally how he or she feels during the meeting. They continuously show if they think the subjects for discussion are interesting and if they agree with the speakers.

The people that are present can determine, without words, how the conversation goes and who gets the floor. It often seems that the people who talk the most have the most influence on the course of the conversation and on the eventual decision–making. However, this is not always the case. Sometimes people who do not have much to say can change or disrupt the course of the conversation just by their presence.

When you are the chairman of such a meeting it is important to be able to interpret the body language of the people who are participating in the meeting. As the chairman, you can use body language techniques to guide the conversation.

Involvement

When the people who are participating in a meeting are discussing a subject, their involvement can be seen from their attitude. The people who are not that interested sit back in their chairs, and often draw the nicest doodles, while giving others the idea that they are taking notes. The people who are really not interested at all stare idly into space or just keep looking around them. When everyone adopts this pose, then it's possible that the meeting was scheduled for the wrong time of the day or there is little interest for the subject. In that case such subjects do not need to be discussed for very long.

People who are participating in the meeting and are of the opinion that the subject is important follow the speakers in a non–verbal manner. When they agree with the speaker, they nod a lot. They take on an open, attentive attitude whereby they often lean forward a little. It is also striking how often listeners adopt the same attitude as the speaker that they are in agreement with. By paying attention to the attitudes of the people present, you can get an idea about the division of opinions. Maybe half of the listeners adopt the attitude of the speaker and the other half is sitting in a defensive attitude. The people who are in disagreement with the speaker hardly move their heads. They sit backwards and adopt a glassy, closed attitude. Often they fold their arms or they cover their mouths with their hands. When they start shaking their heads they are probably about to say something.

Who Gets the Floor?

It is the chairman's task to ensure that everyone who is participating in the meeting all gets the floor proportionally, and that the different points of view as regards a subject are heard. You can also use your knowledge of body language here. When someone wants to say something, he shows this through his breathing. A deep breath is often a sign that someone wants to interrupt the speaker and wants to take the floor. As a leader, it is important to recognise this sign. Eye contact and small gestures with your head and hands are often sufficient to guide the course of the conversation; body contact is screaming. However, sometimes it can be useful to touch someone for a moment to interrupt him or her.

Involve Everyone!

It is important to involve everyone in the meeting. People who are silent also have an opinion, and it is important to hear this opinion during the meeting. It often happens that people are silent during the meeting and only express their opinion afterwards in the corridors. However, people who are silent do react, in a non–verbal manner, on what is being said during the meeting. A good way to involve them in a conversation is by reacting on their body language. You can address the non–verbal behaviour and link a question to it such as: 'I see you are nodding, why do you think it's important that this meeting is carried on?' or 'What a deep sigh, do you have a problem with this statement?'.

Content and Relation

Communication also takes place on a relational level during a meeting, besides the discussions relating to the subjects. It is not so much about what a speaker says exactly but more about what he 'actually' means with what he says. An underlying message can be given for example about the relation with another person in the meeting. The meaning of a comment sometimes becomes clearer through the body language of the speaker than through the words. Especially through variation in intonation and mimics, a statement can have a completely different meaning. As the leader, knowledge of body language can help you recognise this in time and react on it.

Emotional Aspects in the Meeting

In communication between people, our feelings as well as our thoughts are involved. What we think is usually expressed verbally, and what we feel and want during a group activity is usually expressed non–verbally: through blushing, raising your voice, an angry face, surly silence, banging your fist on the table, walking away from a meeting, etc. It is important to recognise the emotional involvement of people and to take into account the influence this can have on other people in the meeting. When a subject of discussion becomes too emotionally charged, sometimes it can be better to defer this point to another meeting. There are people who are quick to react emotionally. Other people can show enormous emotional expression during a meeting, but only with the objective of achieve something. Talking about awareness of body language.... (!)

Body Language During a Job Interview

The rules as regards applying for jobs have been subject to enormous changes lately. In the past, people preferred a hand–written application letter. It is becoming more and more common these days to find a vacancy on the Internet, and to apply for it via the Internet as well. Quite often it is sufficient to place your C.V. on the web. Because of this, the application procedure often goes quicker, and now you can find yourself invited for a job interview before you know it. You can find information on the Internet about how to apply for jobs. Information can be found about how to write your application letter, the clothes that you should wear and how to carry out the interview itself. The importance of body language is often mentioned, but doesn't always get the attention it deserves. After all, before a word has even been spoken, your body language will have already given people their first impression of you.

What Type of Person are You?

By using words you can explain what type of education you have received and what experience you have gained since then. You can also show through words that you know what you're talking about and you can answer questions to clarify matters. At the same time however, your body language will also give out a lot more information. Based on your body language it can be seen if you come across as insecure or self–assured. It can also show if you are a busy or a quiet type and it helps give an impression of whether you are speaking truthfully or not. Body language can show if you not prone to stress. It can show how enthusiastic you are and if you are a nice person, someone who will take his work serious, but also someone who has a sense of humour and can enjoy a joke from time to time. The members of the application committee will ask you questions, but your answers won't only be oral. The committee will not only pay attention to what you say, but also to how you say it! Body language will determine first if it 'clicks', and sometimes all it takes is just a few seconds. Everybody uses body language, but it takes place mostly at a subconscious level. Through becoming more aware of your own body language, but also through recognising the body language of others, you can definitely increase your chances of getting the job.

Ways to Make Your Body Speak

If your platform behaviour includes mannerisms unrelated to your spoken message, those actions will call attention to themselves and away from your speech. Below are provided some ways to use your body language effectively during interviews or Group Discussions.

Rid Yourself of Distracting Mannerisms

Eliminate vocal and visual impediments.

Some common faults of inexperienced or in–effective speakers are:

- Gripping or leaning on the lectern
- Finger tapping
- Lip biting or licking
- Toying with coins or jewellery

- Frowning
- Adjusting hair or clothing
- Head wagging

These have two things in common:

- They are physical manifestations of simple nervousness.
- They are performed unconsciously.

When you make a verbal mistake, you can easily correct it because you can hear your own words, but you can't see yourself, so most distracting mannerisms go uncorrected. You can't eliminate them unless you know they exist.

Videotape Yourself

The first step in eliminating any superfluous behaviour is to obtain an accurate perception of your body's image. This should include:

- Posture
- Gestures
- Body movement
- Facial expressions
- Eye contact

The next step is to free yourself of physical behaviours that do not add to your speech. This can be accomplished by simply becoming aware of your problem areas. After you have videotaped yourself speaking, review the tape several times and make a list of all the distracting mannerisms you notice.

Reviewing Yourself

First review. Review your tape the first time without looking for mannerisms. Just listen to the presentation as if you were hearing it for the first time and evaluate the overall impact you experience from watching the tape.

Second review. Review your tape a second time (with the volume turned down) and look for visual distractions. Take notes on what you observe.

Third review. During this review, have the picture turned off and listen only to your voice. Many people have never even heard a taping of their own voice before. Become accustomed to listening to your voice. Get to know it as others hear it. Note what you like and what you don't like. Pay attention to the speed, the volume and the tone of your voice.

Fourth review. Once you have made lists both of your distracting mannerisms and your more positive points, you are ready to have one or two family members watch the tape with you. Get their initial impression. Ask them to be honest.

Once you have completed these reviews, go over the list of all the distracting mannerisms you saw and heard. The next time you are having a conversation with someone you know well, try to notice whether you use any of these distracting mannerisms even in casual circumstances. Tackle each of your negative points one at a time.

Choosing the Right Seat

After the initial introduction you will usually be directed to take a seat. If you are left to choose a place yourself, choose a place from where you can clearly see all the interview participants, and from where they can also see you. If someone is sitting half behind you, and you can't really see him, he may not get such a good impression of you because of this.

The everyday seating position, with legs crossed high–up is not suitable for the interview setting because in this intimate context it actually conveys a defensive attitude. Your legs need to convey confidence and there are two key positions that can communicate this – the low cross or athletic position. The athletic position is where one leg is brought under your chair so that only the toe of that shoe is in contact with the floor. The other leg is firmly planted on the floor, parallel with the direction of the chair, with the entire sole of that shoe on the floor. This is a powerful position, conveying a readiness for action. The athletic position is often not suited to female clothing and here the low cross position, where the legs are kept together and crossed at the ankles is often the best option.

When should you look at whom?

During the job interview it is important to look at all the interview partners to an equal extent. By looking directly at the other person we are giving them a sign of trust. By looking directly at people we are also in control of the conversation. Looking directly at somebody or looking away actually serves as the dots and commas in our spoken sentences. When one of the committee members explains something or poses a question, keep looking at this person for as long as he or she is speaking. This shows that you're listening. While he is speaking he may also look at the other people, but every time he wants to emphasise something he will look at you again. You can then nod to encourage him to continue talking. At the end of his question, he will keep looking at you and then tilt his head up a little to invite you to give an answer. When you answer a question, you will look first at the person who posed the question, but while you answer you should take turns looking at the other interview partners as well. You should direct yourself again to the person who posed the question when you want to emphasise something and at the end of your answer.

Pay attention to the body language of interview partners

Apart from paying attention to your own body language, it is also important to see how your interview partners are behaving. The postures and movements of other people can give you an impression of how you are coming across to them. This can serve as a warning at an early stage that you might be doing something wrong that you are not being aware of. For example, when the committee members are of the opinion that you hold the floor for too long or you annoy them with your interruptions, they will show their irritation at first through their body language. When the committee members shake their heads, sigh or fold their arms and lean back, you can take this as a sign of displeasure. Usually it is not yet too late to change this. You see, it also applies to your interview partners that their body language takes place subconsciously. However, don't wait too long because then their irritation will transfer to their consciousness.

Do not worry too much about tension

Knowledge of body language can help you improve the mutual tuning during the interview. You can use this knowledge to hide your nervousness a little, but actually this is something you shouldn't worry about too much. Many applicants are nervous during an interview and of course they would much prefer not to let this nervousness show. However, it's not such a bad thing to be nervous. The committee members will understand this. Your nervousness may even show that you feel this job is important to you. If you weren't nervous, and therefore sit a little nonchalant, it might indicate that you are not that interested. Also realise that the job interview is more than just a means for the employer to determine which of the candidates is most suitable for the job. The job interview especially is a moment of mutual acquaintance. It's a first meeting with people that you might soon work together with. Therefore the boss should actually be just as nervous as you!

Watch the Way You Walk

Moving forces people to focus and follow you. The way you walk from your seat to the speaker's position is very important. When you are introduced, you should appear eager to speak.

Too many speakers look as though they are heading towards execution.

Walk confidently from your seat to the lectern. Pause there for a few seconds, then move out from behind the lectern. As discussed before, it is wise to use the lectern as a point of departure and not a barrier to hide behind.

Smile before you say your first words. Be careful not to stand too close to, nor move beyond, the people in the front row. Be careful not to walk too much. Doing so will work against you. Continuous pacing is distracting. Walking can be an effective way to stress an important idea. It is essential that your walk be purposeful and intentional, not just a random shift of position. Taking about three steps, moving at a shallow angle, usually works best.

When employing visual aids, use three positions. One position is your 'home' position and should be front and centre. The other two positions should be relatively near the 'home' position. Never stand in front of any visual aid.

When you practice your speaking, make sure you also practice your walking patterns. Try walking to and from your three positions. These positions should be planned just as your hand gestures are.

When standing still, remember to maintain good posture. Stand up straight.

Remember: It is not what you say it is how you say it and your body does speak very loudly. It is only when you marry your verbal message and you nonverbal message does a speaker begin to command presence.

Aspects of Body Language

Body language is a very important part of any communication.

It will be analyzed by the interviewer; even if they are unaware of this at the conscious level. A brilliantly prepared interview delivered in an interesting voice will fall well short of the mark if accompanied by negative, intrusive or hostile body language. There are three main aspects of body language that you should consider: what to do with your eyes, what your facial expressions indicate and the positioning and movement of your torso and limbs.

Mirroring

In any intimate communication there is a natural tendency to mirror the pose and position of the person you are talking to, and this behaviour tends to result in a more relaxed and agreeable atmosphere. You can help to put the interviewer at ease by being aware of this and making a positive but subtle effort to mirror their body language. The concept of mirroring is based on the well–known human trait of like attracting like. People generally like people that appear to be similar to them. Therefore, by observing the interviewers body language and reflecting this back at them they are likely to feel more at ease and friendly towards you. An individual's facial expression, tone of voice, body posture and movement often convey a world of detail about what they are thinking and feeling and how they are reacting to what you are saying. The effective use and interpretation of body language communication will help you to identify subtle aspects of the interviewer's attitudes and reactions. This understanding and interpretation of body language is a key component of intelligent listening.

Maintaining LPM

As most interviews are held with both parties seated it is important to convey a positive message in the way you sit. In particular, this comes down to the placement of your arms and legs. With the upper limbs the guideline is that the less a person moves their hands and arms, the more powerful they are. This supports the view that they are used to people listening to them and they therefore do not have to resort to gesticulation to get their point across. The technical term for this is Low Peripheral Movement, or LPM. When being interviewed, maintain LPM and you will make a more impressive impact with your interviewer. Try to keep your hands lower than your elbows; rest them on the arms of the chair, your thighs or even make a low steeple with the fingers of both hands.

Eye Contact

Eye contact is the cement that binds together speakers and their audiences. When you speak, your eyes involve your listeners in your presentation. There is no surer way to break a communication bond between you and the audience than by failing to look at your listeners. No matter how large your audience may be, each listener wants to feel that you are talking to him or her.

The adage, 'The eyes are the mirror of the soul,' underlines the need for you to convince people with your eyes, as well as your words. Only by looking at your listeners as individuals can you convince them that you are sincere and are interested in them and that you care whether they accept your message. When you speak, your eyes also function as a control device you can use to assure your listeners' attentiveness and concentration.

Eye contact can also help you to overcome nervousness by making your audience a known quantity. Effective eye contact is an important feedback device that makes the speaking situation a two–way communication process. By looking at your audience, you can determine how they are reacting. When you develop the ability to gauge the audience's reactions and adjust your presentation accordingly, you will be a much more effective speaker.

Understanding where to look to make positive eye contact is only part of the story. You also need to know how and when to use this non–verbal communication. The amount of eye contact you make should differ fundamentally depending on whether you are in the role of speaker or listener. It is in the role of listener that you should instigate more eye contact and hold it for longer periods of time. It supports your role as an attentive listener, whereas overusing eye contact when speaking may appear a demand for the interviewer to pay attention. As a speaker holding eye contact initially for 5 to 10 seconds and after that using it in an intermittent way is ideal. This way you do not appear to be lecturing or hectoring and the listener does not feel that they are being challenged to a staring contest. It is normal for the listener to maintain eye contact for longer than the speaker who will typically break off and then revisit this form of contact as they are speaking. Eye contact when used positively can be a very effective form of non–verbal communication. However, excessive or inappropriate eye contact will prevent you establishing a good relationship with your interviewer.

Body Language Do's and Don'ts

Do

- Sit up straight, and lean slightly forward in your chair. In addition to projecting interest and engagement in the interaction, aligning your body's position to that of the interviewer's shows admiration and agreement.
- Show your enthusiasm by keeping an interested expression. Nod and make positive gestures in moderation to avoid looking like a bobblehead.
- Establish a comfortable amount of personal space between you and the interviewer. Invading personal space (anything more than 20 inches) could make the interviewer feel

uncomfortable and take the focus away from your conversation.

- Limit your application of colognes and perfumes. Invading aromas can arouse allergies. Being the candidate that gave the interviewer a headache isn't going to do anything in your favour.
- If you have more than one person interviewing you at once, make sure you briefly address both people with your gaze (without looking like a tennis spectator) and return your attention to the person who has asked you a question.
- Interruptions can happen. If they do, refrain from staring at your interviewer while they address their immediate business and motion your willingness to leave if they need privacy.
- Stand up and smile even if you are on a phone interview. Standing increases your level of alertness and allows you to become more engaged in the conversation.

Don't

- Rub the back of your head or neck. Even if you really do just have a cramp in your neck, these gestures make you look disinterested.
- Rub or touch your nose. This suggests that you're not being completely honest, and it's gross.
- Sit with your armed folded across your chest. You'll appear unfriendly and disengaged.
- Cross your legs and idly shake one over the other. It's distracting and shows how uncomfortable you are.
- Lean your body towards the door. You'll appear ready to make a mad dash for the door.
- Slouch back in your seat. This will make you appear disinterested and unprepared.

- Stare back blankly. This is a look people naturally adapt when they are trying to distance themselves.

Body Language Traits

Have a quick look at these common body language traits:

Gesture	Meaning
Arms crossed on chest	Defensiveness
Head tilted	Interested
Touching nose	Rejection, denial
Pupils of eye dilated	Interest
Unbuttoned coat	Agreeableness receptivity
Unbuttoned shirts	Aggressiveness
Hand before mouth	Uncertainty/insincerity
Hand along cheek	Contemplation, evaluation
Joined finger tips	Confidence, pride
Excessive blinking	Anxiety
Rubbing back of neck	Frustration
Leaning forward	Interest
Stroking chin	Evaluation, judgement
Leaning backward	Reserved judgement

Chapter 15

Dressing for a GD

Group Discussions have become a common feature in MBA entrance exams. Apart from gearing up their skills to be effective in discussions and minding the way their body speaks, they are also required to dress according to the occasion. We've all heard the expression, 'You have only one chance to make a good first impression.' How true that is! One of the main purposes of an interview is to present yourself to a potential employer in a manner that reflects a highly polished and professional image. It is important to keep in mind that the interview is not the time to be making a personal statement with the way you dress. Your goal should be to show that you respect the interviewer's values, tastes, and expectations relative to dress and personal manner.

What Your Clothes Say About You

In an interview your attire plays a supporting role. Your conduct, your interpersonal skills and your ability to articulate intelligent and well thought out responses to questions are the most important elements. Appropriate attire supports your image as a person who takes the interview process seriously and understands the nature of the industry in which you are trying to become employed.

Be aware that in some industries, customer contact and image presented to the customer is critical. In such industries, your attire will be judged more critically. Your attire should be noticed as being appropriate and well–fitting, but it should not take centre stage.

If you are primarily remembered for your interview attire, this is probably because you made an error in judgment! Dressing nicely and appropriately is a compliment to the person you meet, so if in doubt, err on the side of dressing better than you might need to. Even if you are aware that employees of an organisation dress casually on the job, dress up for the interview or GD unless you are specifically told otherwise by the employer. Never confuse an interview or business function with a social event. Don't dress for a party or a date. Not every contact with an employer requires interview attire. For some occasions, business casual is appropriate.

Although professional dress and appropriate style may vary slightly depending on job type, work environment and geographical region, there are several key points to keep in mind.

Attire for Men

- A conservative business suit is almost always the rule. A well–tailored or fitted suit coat and trousers will go a long way in helping you present yourself professionally and confidently. For example, coat sleeve and trouser length should be such that the fit is neither too short nor too long. Appropriate size is critical not only for comfort, but also for presenting a 'clean' fit. There is no room for sloppiness. Although new graduates are often working with a tight personal budget, shopping for a new suit at a discount–clothing outlet is generally not suggested. The additional expense invested in a quality suit will pay tremendous dividends in making a positive first impression and serve to enhance your confidence.
- Acceptable colours continue to be darker shades and hues including greys, blues (navy), and black. Pattern designs

such as pin stripes and plaids are acceptable as long as they are subtle. In warmer climates there is generally more leniency toward lighter shades of blues, greys, and even tan. Likewise, lightweight fabrics are more practical in the south while wool or wool blends are commonplace in northern climates. A general rule of thumb is to stay away from the browns and greens...these colours are more acceptable at a football game on a cold day, grey or on the golf course on a bright, sunny morning!

- A plain white or off–white shirt is always a winner. In most cases, either a loose or button–down collar (oxford cloth) is fine. Occasionally pastel shades (blue, pink, yellow, etc.) are acceptable, as is a pin–stripe design as long as the look is conservative and not flashy.
- Neckties...again the word is conservative. Patterns should be uniform and subtle, whether stripes or small dots. Paisley designs are generally acceptable. Deep reds, maroon, blues, navy, greys and black are colours that blend well with dark suits, once again keeping in mind that slight variations may occur due to region and climate. Width should generally be about the same as your coat lapels.
- Dressing in your best attire for the interview also means having your shoes shined, if not new. Wearing a new suit and tie with an old, dirty pair of shoes would be like washing and waxing your car without scrubbing the tires and hubcaps. Laced shoes are the general rule; loafers are a little too casual, and hush puppies should be reserved for Friday night barbecues. The colour of your socks should complement or match the rest of your outfit. Argyle and see–through socks are not considered appropriate. Likewise, a leather belt that matches the colour of your shoes and has a small buckle is a good choice.

Attire For Women

- Dressing in a conservative business suit is the best way to present a professional image. The suit should fit well and make you feel good about yourself.
- Studies in social psychology have shown that women have an advantage over men when it comes to selecting colours for professional dress. Although the greys and blues are standard, women tend to be able to get away with wearing more of a variety of colours. Oftentimes, bright colours including reds, maroon, various shades of blue and even green are acceptable. Women are also usually able to wear various fabrics without appearing unprofessional.
- Your blouse should complement the suit in a conservative fashion. It should not be too revealing, high around the neck, nor have too many ruffles or frills. White or off–white colours such as cream usually match well with many suit colours. See-through blouses are discouraged for the professional interview.
- Stockings are a must and should be flesh–toned or of a colour very close to it. Avoid colour or patterns that would be distracting.
- Shoes should be sensibly selected in a way that is not intended to make a statement. High heels and open toes are choices better left for activities other than the professional interview.
- If you carry a purse, keep it small and simple, especially if you also carry a briefcase. Purse colour should coordinate with your shoes. You may choose to carry a small briefcase or business–like tote bag in place of a purse. Leather is the best choice for briefcases; micro fiber or fine wovens are also acceptable.
- Wear a conservative watch. Jewellery and scarf styles come

and go. Keep your choices simple and leaning toward conservative. Avoid extremes of style and colour. If your industry is creative, you may have more flexibility than someone pursuing a conservative industry.

- Keep the makeup conservative. A little is usually better than none for a polished look. Nails should be clean and well groomed. Avoid extremes of nail length and polish colour, especially in conservative industries.

Some Rules for both for Men and Women

- Hair should be of a conservative style and not look like you have spent hours caring for it. The currently popular dishevelled hairstyles may not be the best way to make points with a professional interviewer. Men who wear beards and mustaches should take extra time to make sure facial hair is neatly trimmed and not too long. Women can usually wear their hair in more styles as long as it is not too wild and brash. Fingernails should be trimmed and hands clean. Women should not go overboard with bright, flashy nail polish colours, and lipstick and eye makeup should be used moderately.
- Jewellery should be kept to a minimum and conservative in appearance. Gold medallions and sparkling chains are better left for downtown clubs, wedding receptions, and masquerade parties. Women should not wear giant hoop earrings or ones that are extremely flashy. Likewise, don't wear too many rings...one or two are plenty.
- Cologne and perfume are fine for both men and women as long as it is not overbearing. You don't want to knock someone over by using a half bottle of aftershave or perfume.

CHAPTER 16

Group Discussions FAQs

Here are some frequently asked questions by MBA candidates aspiring to appear for Group Discussions.

Should we begin the GD by appointing a leader amongst ourselves?

No, you should not. Leadership in a GD is established implicitly through one's performance in the GD.

What is the normal duration of a GD?

A GD is generally of 15–20 minutes duration.

Am I allowed to carry a piece of paper during the GD for noting down important points?

Normally you are allowed to carry a piece of paper, but there might be some instances where you are specifically forbidden.

How many panel members are there to evaluate?

There are usually 3–4 panel members to evaluate.

Is there time given for preparation after the topic is given and before starting the GD?

Usually some time (2–5 minutes) is given to collect one's thoughts, but there could be instances when this does not happen, so it is best not to bank on this.

Is there any particular seating arrangement that is favourable for the participants?

If the participants are asked to sit in a circle or a semi–circle, one position is as good as the other. But at times you are asked to sit on either side of a rectangular table, a position as close to the centre as possible would be favourable.

Is it true that the person who speaks the most in a GD is the one who is most successful?

This is a myth. Generally, the person who has a sound knowledge of the topic and is a clear thinker speaks more. This leads the students into believing that whoever speaks most is successful. But, just speaking for the sake of speaking will not take you far.

Can I take a definite stand during the start of the GD and later on during the GD switch over to the other side of the argument?

Yes, provided you do it in the right way. In a GD it is quite likely that you get convinced by some other participant's counter–argument to your point. If this happens, then it is best if you accept his argument and explain to the group how your previous argument was true within a narrow range, and how the new argument is applicable to a broader range. This also gives an indicator of your flexibility and acceptance of another's point of view. Naturally, it is safe not to make any rash statements or go against the topic before you learn the facts of the argument. Blindly taking a stand will definitely lead you into trouble. This does not mean that you should sit on the fence. You may participate actively by pointing out issues on both sides of the argument in a responsible and logical manner.

If I do not understand the meaning of the topic, should I ask the moderator to explain it?

You cannot ask the moderator the meaning of the topic. Instead of displaying your ignorance in this manner, it is better to wait for some other participant to initiate the discussion. So, listen to the discussion carefully for the first three or four minutes, and when you have gained some idea about the topic, participate in the discussion.

Should I address the other participants by their names or by their signified numbers?

You should avoid the use of numbers. You can use names. It shows you have taken effort to know people in the group, but do not make the mistake of calling a person by some other name by mistake. It is better to use pronouns such as 'he', 'she', 'you', etc. while referring to the other members of your group. Phrases like 'my friend here' can be used occasionally but not frequently as it sounds very patronizing.

Can I use a language other than English to drive home my point?

No. You will have to stick to English.

Which is the right time to enter a GD to ensure that I am heard properly?

In any GD, there are crests and troughs during the discussion. At a crest, the noise level is the maximum and at a trough there is almost total silence. Ideally, you should enter the GD during the trough period but normally in competitive GDs the crests occur more often and for more prolonged periods. Troughs, if they do come, last for very little time. In such cases, you could identify those stages in the GD where ideas familiar to you are being discussed and enter the GD irrespective of the noise level.

How do I participate when the noise level is too high?

If the noise level is high, you have two options – remain silent, or join in by raising your voice to be heard above the din. You need to be firm and ensure that your voice is strong enough to be heard clearly. However, it is important to understand the difference between being firm and shouting. Do not ever raise your voice loud enough to be classified as 'shouter'.

Should I encourage others to speak up?

Do not directly put someone who is consistently silent on the spot by asking him/her to speak up. If someone has been trying to speak and has a good point but is cut off constantly, you may encourage him/her to continue with her point as you would like to hear her out.

Are the group members supposed to keep track of the time or will the panel keep track?

It would be good if you are conscious of the time, but not to the point of getting so distracted looking at your watch that you do not contribute to the discussion.

For how long should I participate?

In a 20 minute GD with 12 – 15 participants, you should participate at least four times with each entry lasting for at least 20 – 25 seconds. You could participate more depending upon your comfort level and the need for participation.

Is the use of slang/colloquialism permitted?

It is best to avoid using slangs.

How important is the use of body language in a GD?

Use of proper body language is an advantage. Some of the ways in which you could use your body effectively are:

- Have significant eye contact. Look at the GD members when you speak to them. Focus on the whole group and not on specific individuals.

- Keep your body upright, and lean forward while speaking or listening. This will show your sustained interest in the GD.
- If you agree with somebody, nod your head, so that the speaker realises that you understand him.
- Use your hands effectively to emphasise your statements and to persuade others to listen to you. Do not gesture wildly, but use your hands as a means of communication.
- Do not place your hand in front of your mouth while speaking. It inhibits speech and shows self–consciousness.
- Do not use your arm to support your chin. It communicates a lack of interest in the GD.
- Do not point your finger or pen at anyone aggressively. These are intimidating tactics and will be recognised as such.
- Keep your hands on the table when you are not using them to emphasise your points. If you tend to keep your hands moving then you might end up distracting others.

What do I do if someone else has already said all that I wanted to say?

You have two choices:

- Agree with the point made by your colleague and add on to it by displaying the applicability of the argument to different situations. By doing this you will have broadened the scope of the argument.
- Drop the point and think of something new to say.

What are the acceptable ways of interrupting somebody else, so that I may make my point?

- By saying, 'Excuse me, but I feel that what you are saying is not totally true…'

- By saying, 'Yes, I agree with your idea, and I would like to add on to it…'
- By asking for some clarification from the speaker on the point which he is making at that moment.

Should we make an interim summary?

An interim summary is a way of directing the group mid-way through the GD. It helps the group to pick out and focus on the most important points and thus use the remaining time more effectively. However, it is not necessary to make an interim summary, if the discussion is already well focused.

How is aggression taken and measured in a GD?

The moment you notice people reacting to you negatively or strongly, you may take it that you are being too aggressive. The degree of the reaction is the measure of your aggression.

What level of aggression is seen acceptable?

There is a very thin line between aggression and assertiveness. You should always aim to sound assertive and not stubborn.

Is it true that the GD is used more as an elimination technique rather than as a selection tool?

Depends on the institute. In most premier institutes it is used as a selection tool, not as an elimination technique.

What is the level of accuracy desired in the facts and figures you quote during the GD?

An error margin of 5% is acceptable.

Does the moderator have any biases or preconceived notions about the topic?

Ideally the moderator is supposed to be unbiased and neutral. But, being a human being, the moderator cannot be totally free from bias. Since this is not a factor within your control, there isn't much point losing sleep over it.

Can we expect the moderator to stop or cut short the GD much before the stipulated time is over?

This may happen if the GD becomes too noisy and if the level of discussion deteriorates abysmally.

Is it necessary that a group should arrive at a conclusion in the stipulated time?

Ideally a group is supposed to reach a conclusion. Normally the time constraints do not allow the group to do so.

Is an end-summary absolutely essential?

No. If the group has not reached a conclusion, then it would be good if someone puts the whole discussion into perspective by summarizing. But, if there isn't sufficient time, a summary may be avoided.

Is voting an acceptable method of reaching a consensus?

Certainly not. A GD is not a debate.

Chapter 17

Mock Group Discussion

Most topics in Group Discussions are taken from the current political or economic scene. So, if one has just kept abreast of current affairs, then he will be able to make a mark. Have a look at a group discussion on a common topic.

Judge: Good morning. You can choose any topic you like or take a slip from that box. You are given one minute to think to start with the discussion. The observers will not interfere in your discussion. If no conclusion is reached, we may ask each of you to speak for a minute on the topic at the end of the discussion.

The topic on the slip is

'Multinationals: Bane or Boon'. I suggest you should start the discussion.

Tarun: This is a good topic. I am against multinationals. We have Coke and Pepsi. Do we need them? We can manufacture our own soft drinks. Multinationals destroy the local industry and sell non–essential products.

Hemant: I agree with you. What is the fun of having Coke and Pepsi? We have our own Campa Cola.

Shishir: I think water is good enough.

Dhruv: We are not here to discuss soft drinks. The topic given to us is a much larger one. First, let us define multinational companies. They are merely large companies which operate in a number of countries. There could be some Indian multinationals also. So, there is nothing wrong with them. The point is whether they have a good or bad impact on the host countries. We have to discuss their business practices and find out whether they are desirable or not.

Raghav: That is a very good introduction to the topic. Multinational companies do serve an important function of bringing new products and technologies in countries which do not have them. And, it is not just Coke and Pepsi. They set up power plants and build roads and bridges which really help in the development of host countries.

Amit: But are they all that good? We have seen that they destroy local industry. In India they just took over existing companies. They came in areas of low technology. Moreover, we have to see why they come at all. They come for earning profits and often remit more money abroad than they bring in.

Tarun: I agree with you. I am against multinationals. We can produce everything ourselves. We should be swadeshi in our approach. Why do we need multinational companies?

Raghav: We may not need multinational companies but then it also means that our companies should not do business abroad. Can we live in an isolated world? The fact is that we are moving towards becoming a global village. The world is interconnected.

Then, we have also seen that foreign companies bring in business practices that we are impressed with. Look at foreign banks. They are so efficient and friendly that the nationalised banks look pathetic in comparison. I think we can learn a lot from multinationals if we keep our eyes and mind open.

Hemant: Take a look at McDonalds. They are providing quality meals at affordable prices. One does not have to wait at their restaurants.

Shishir: But, my friend, how do you account for the fact that they take out more than they put in and thus lead to impoverishing the country?

Dhruv: The fact is that every poor country needs foreign investment. Poor countries often lack resources of their own. That is why they have to invite foreign companies in. There is nothing wrong in this because then products like cars, air conditioners and so on can be made in poor countries. Often multinationals source products from different countries which helps boost their export earnings.

Raghav: We have been talking about Coke and Pepsi. It is well known that Pepsi is in the foods business also and has helped farmers in Punjab by setting up modern farms to grow potatoes and tomatoes. Modern practices have helped the people in that area.

Tarun: But, I still feel that multinationals are harmful for the country.

Dhruv: Well, there could be negative things associated with such companies. They may not be very good in their practices. But, can we do without them? I think the best way is to invite them but also impose some controls so that they follow the laws of the country and do not indulge in unfair practices.

Raghav: I think laws are applicable to everyone. Very often officials in poor countries take bribes. The fault lies not with the company which gives a bribe but the person who actually demands one. Why blame the companies for our own ills?

Tarun: What about the money they take out?

Dhruv : We have had a good discussion and I think it is time to sum up.

Multinationals may have good points and some bad ones too, but competition is never harmful for anyone. We cannot live in a protected economy any longer. We have been protected for many years and the results are there for everyone to see. Rather than be close about multinationals, let us invite them in selected areas so that we get foreign investment in areas which we are lacking. Laws can be strictly enforced that companies operate within limits and do not start meddling in political affairs.

Analysis: Though Tarun started the discussion, he could not make any good points. Later, he could not give any points about why multinationals are bad. It is also a bad strategy to say at the outset whether you are for or against the topic. Remember, it is not a debate but a discussion. The first step should always be to introduce the topic without taking sides. See the way in which the discussion is proceeding and give arguments for or against. The observer is not interested in your beliefs but in what you are saying. The participation of Hemant and Shishir is below average. A candidate must make 3–4 interventions.

Their arguments are also not well thought out and add nothing to the discussion. It is important to say relevant things which make an impact rather than speak for the sake of speaking. The arguments of Dhruv and Raghav are better. They seem to be aware of the role of multinational companies. Raghav's approach is better, as he intervenes a number of times. He has also taken initiative in the beginning and brought order to the group. If selection has to be made from the above six candidates, the obvious choice would be Raghav and thereafter, Dhruv.

Points that are Observed

- Leadership skills
- Confidence
- Consideration for others
- Manners
- Aggressive behaviour
- Substantial viewpoints vs. frivolous viewpoints

■■■